BECAUSE OF
JESUS

The Persecution of the Prophets

P. James

ISBN: 978-1-910719-68-8

Published for P. James by
Verité CM Limited,
124 Sea Place, Worthing, West Sussex BN12 4BG
+44 (0) 1903 241975

email: enquiries@veritecm.com
Web: www.veritecm.com

British Library Cataloguing in Publication Data
A catalogue record for this book is available from the British Library

Design and Typesetting by Verité CM Ltd

Printed in England

'Brothers and sisters, as an example of

patience in the face of suffering,

take the prophets who spoke

in the name of the Lord.'

(James 5: 10)

CONTENTS

INTRODUCTION

'REJOICE AND BE GLAD'

Now when Jesus saw the crowds, he went up on a mountainside and sat down. His disciples came to him, and he began to teach them. He said... "Blessed are those who are persecuted because of righteousness, for theirs is the kingdom of heaven. Blessed are you when people insult you, persecute you and falsely say all kinds of evil against you because of me. Rejoice and be glad, because great is your reward in heaven, for in the same way they persecuted the prophets who were before you. (Matthew 5: 1-2, 10-12)

This is an extract from the beginning of what is popularly called the Sermon on the Mount, the longest recorded sermon of the LORD Jesus Christ. The Sermon starts with the LORD setting out the blessings of God the Father: they are given to those who are poor in spirit, merciful, pure in heart, peacemakers etc. The LORD then added that blessing is also given to those who are persecuted. Anyone who suffers evil because of Christ is blessed. Indeed, His disciples should 'Rejoice and be glad' if they are persecuted because of Him or, as Christ's words are recorded in the book of Luke, they should 'leap for joy'[1].

---

1   Luke 6: 22-23

Christ's message is that it is part of the calling of His disciples to be persecuted, but they will be blessed through it.

Why? Why is it a blessing to be persecuted? Why is it a cause of rejoicing? Because to experience opposition for the sake of Christ binds us ever closer to Him; it strips back our own self-dependency and helps us to be like Christ, trusting in His Father, and fully enjoying His love and mercy. It is when the world opposes us because of Christ that we can feel closest to the Father. Christ is not saying we will enjoy suffering but that at times of persecution we will know the joy of His Father's care. That is to be blessed.

In making His point, the LORD Jesus added that when His disciples are persecuted because of Him, they are following in the footsteps of the Old Testament prophets, who were persecuted 'in the same way'. The LORD was making clear that it was because of Him that the prophets experienced insults, persecution and slander. The prophets were persecuted because of Christ. Anyone who is persecuted now for Christ's sake has the privilege of being like the prophets. And together with them, the LORD added, you will receive a great reward in heaven.

Christ was calling His disciples to be like the prophets – to follow their example of suffering because of Him. 'Because of *Him*'. Christ presumed that the prophets trusted in *Him* as LORD; not in Baal or the gods of the Canaanites or in a mysterious, impersonal 'one God'. If the ancient prophets had believed in any such god it is probable they would not have been persecuted. No, they suffered because they trusted in the LORD Jesus – the Eternal Son of the Father, united in the Holy Spirit. They believed that the LORD alone revealed the true and living God. They were persecuted because their faith in the LORD Jesus testified that no other god is God.

Hence the Psalmist cries, 'If we had forgotten the name of our God or spread out our hands to a foreign god, would not God have discovered it, since he knows the secrets of the heart? Yet for your sake we face death all day long; we are considered as sheep to be slaughtered' (Psalm 44: 20-22). It was because the Church was trusting in the LORD Jesus that they were being persecuted. It was for *His* sake. And the Church cried to Him to save them: 'Rise up and help us; rescue us because of your unfailing love' (v26).

The apostle Paul instructs us to share this example of faith in Christ in the face of suffering:

> Who shall separate us from the love of Christ? Shall trouble or hardship or persecution or famine or nakedness or danger or sword? As it is written:
>
> 'For your sake we face death all day long; we are considered as sheep to be slaughtered.' [Psalm 44:22]
>
> No, in all these things we are more than conquerors through him who loved us. For I am convinced that neither death nor life, neither angels nor demons, neither the present nor the future, nor any powers, neither height nor depth, nor anything else in all creation, will be able to separate us from the love of God that is in Christ Jesus our Lord. (Romans 8: 31-39)

This Book

This book examines some of what the Triune God says in the Bible about the way that the prophets were persecuted for the sake of Christ. *Why were they ill-treated? How did their theology help them when they faced insults, abuse or death? How did the true and living God react to their plight?*

It's worth making three points about what the book is and is not about. First, it is about the *persecution* of the prophets. It is not about how they survived more general suffering (illness, famine) or about their experience of discipline or judgement.

Second, the book is about what happens to the *prophets*. This does not mean, however, that it is just about the fate of bearded fellows who roam the desert, denouncing their political and religious leaders. There is clearly within the Bible a distinct office of prophet but all those who live for Christ and witness to Him can be said to be prophets. In the book of 1 Chronicles[2], the LORD referred to the whole Church as His prophets. Moses wished 'all the Lord's people were prophets and that the Lord would put His Spirit on them!' (Numbers 11: 29). The LORD Jesus called Abel a prophet (Luke 11: 51) even though the Bible does not record him speaking at all. But, as we shall see, his actions speak of his faith in Christ – and it was for that reason his blood was spilt.

Third, any book about persecution must also focus on those committing it – the persecutors. What motivated their actions? Why did they behave as they did? Are persecutors in a different category of human being from those they persecute or fundamentally the same? What was their fate having persecuted God's people?

This book is written from the comfort of a land where the Church faces relatively little persecution. Individual Christians, especially converts from certain religious backgrounds, may suffer very greatly. But in general the Church can undertake its work with considerable freedom.

---

2   1 Chronicles 16: 19-22 cf Psalm 105: 12-15

This does not stop some members of the Church within the United Kingdom getting outraged about the tiniest slight or opposition, which confirms their view that this 'once great Christian nation' is going to the dogs.

It's not entirely clear what it is at the heart of this exaggeration of the persecution experienced by Christians: perhaps there is an element of self-righteousness which creates a sense of victimhood. But over-playing our suffering conveniently avoids facing up to the sobering question of whether the Church in the United Kingdom experiences such little persecution because its witness to the LORD Jesus is so poor than there is no need for anyone to oppose it. Furthermore, any over-exaggeration of the Church's persecution in this country serves to weaken sympathy for the real horrors that Christians in other parts of the world are facing.

It is quite possible that over the coming decades the Christian Church in the United Kingdom will face greater trials. But for now, its existence is very peaceful compared to the extreme persecution that Christians are experiencing in many parts of the world. Torture, rape, exile, murder: these are the threats faced daily by our brothers and sisters in Christ.

It would have been easy to include some specific examples of such suffering in this book. Yet contemporary reports become outdated the minute they are written down. The LORD Himself does not let any injustice be forgotten. But, sadly, from a human perspective, the relevance of any story of the Church's persecution soon becomes dated. Rather than add 'current' stories, therefore, I have included in each chapter more generalised accounts of Christians' persecution, leaving room for the reader to think and pray about those to whom they may be applicable. Many readers may be experiencing persecution themselves. The book does not and cannot provide pastoral advice to their specific situation. But it will, I hope, speak something to them in their troubles.

For although today's news speaks to us only for a short while, the Bible remains relevant to every generation. The Bible teaches that, through the Spirit of Christ sent by God the Father, the ancient Scriptures are not old words but living ones. The true and living God calls us to heed what was said a long time ago as He speaks it to us now. We are to hear Christ's voice 'Today', as it was heard many 1000s of years ago 'Today'.[3]

In the Scriptures we read of those who lived before Christ's incarnation; those who lived after He took flesh and met Him in His time on earth; and those who lived after He ascended back to heaven. But the LORD Jesus has always been the one and only Mediator between the true and living God and humanity.[4] What we read in the ancient Scriptures is relevant to the Church now because we are part of the same Church, serving the same Lord – the Eternal Son of God the Father, united in the Holy Spirit. What those Scriptures record about the Old Testament Church was written deliberately for the network of local churches that exists across the world today. The stories in the Law and the Prophets about the faith of the ancient Church in the LORD Jesus were written by the Holy Spirit to encourage the faith of the Church in the LORD Jesus now – in every

---

3 See Hebrews chapter 3 and 4: 1-13

4 See Joel 2: 32, Romans 10: 9-21, 1 Timothy 2: 5, Hebrews 13: 8.

place it exists across the world.[5] The Old Testament speaks to the Church about every type of persecution it faces today.

The apostle Paul, when quoting from the Psalms a prophecy about the persecution of Christ, says that, 'Everything that was written in the past was written to teach us, so that through the endurance taught in the Scriptures and the encouragement they provide we might have hope'.[6] As the LORD Jesus Christ's brother, James, says, when urging his hearers to be patient and stand firm until the LORD's coming, 'Brothers and sisters, as an example of patience in the face of suffering, take the prophets who spoke in the name of the Lord'[7].

The prophets were persecuted because of Christ. The concern of this book is to learn what was written in the Scriptures about their persecution, so that readers will want to follow their example of faith in Christ when we also suffer for His sake.

---

5   The titles 'Jesus' and 'Christ' are ones used in relation to the LORD – the Second Person of the Trinity – after His incarnation. Yet the Bible writers also name the pre-incarnate LORD as Jesus and Christ, and this book follows that precedent. See John 12: 37-41, 1 Corinthians 10: 1-4, Hebrews 11: 26.

6   Romans 15: 3-4 quoting Psalm 69: 9. See also 1 Corinthians 10: 1-13 where Paul also makes clear that what happened to the ancient Church was specifically written down as examples and warnings for the Church in every generation

7   James 5: 7-10

CHAPTER ONE

PERSECUTION WITHIN THE FAMILY

Much of the persecution which is inflicted on Christians is undertaken by members of their own family. For some believers this will take the form of ridicule. Others face much greater suffering: converts from some religions experience alienation from their families; expulsion from their homes; bribery to 'reconvert'; violent threats to renounce their 'apostasy'; and death itself.

The very first story in the Bible about persecution involves two brothers: Cain and Abel. Through the narrative the Holy Spirit teaches us about the suffering Christians can expect from family members who do not share their faith in Christ. The natural inclination of those against Christ is antipathy towards those who love and trust Him, however close their blood ties.

The study is on Genesis 4.

Abel and the Seed

We are told little about the life of Abel; the Scriptures record nothing that he said so we cannot tell what he believed from his words. But we can be confident that his parents, Adam and Eve, taught him all that we read in the early chapters of Genesis. They would have confessed how they had been led by the devil to question whether the

LORD Jesus was God[1], and how they turned their backs on Him, bringing down on them and the whole creation the curse of decay and death.

Yet Adam and Eve would have surely also told Abel how the LORD Jesus had been sent to them by God the Father to prophesy that the power of Satan would be overcome, telling the serpent that:

> I will put enmity between you and the woman, and between your offspring [Seed] and hers; he will crush your head, and you will strike his heel (Genesis 3: 15)

Adam and Eve would have shared the good news about the Son – the Seed 'who is Christ'[2] – who was to be born of a woman, without a human father. There was to be a war between the Seed and Satan but Christ would ultimately crush Satan despite the sufferings He would endure at the hand of His enemy. Satan would 'strike his heel'. The Seed would experience great anguish; but then there would be glory as He destroyed the wicked serpent and won victory over decay and death. The Seed would be united to His Bride – taking on her shame – and would die for Her so there could be life.

The LORD Jesus was going to win the war but it was to be a real war, with tangible and intense suffering. Darkness would try to conquer the Light of the world. Death would seek to overcome the Lord of Life. The Liar would attempt to vanquish the One who is the Truth. Violence would try to destroy the Prince of Peace.

---

1   See Genesis 3 where Eve was deceived by the snake's cunning and led astray from devotion to the LORD Jesus Christ (cf 2 Corinthians 11: 3); and Adam failed to trust the LORD Jesus and exercise his authority over Eve and the snake.

2   Galatians 3: 16 cf v29). The Seed is the hope of the Old Testament church (see, for example, Genesis 12: 7; 13:15; 22: 18, 24: 7).

The LORD's prophecy also foretold that humanity would be caught up in this war, depending on whether they are a follower of Jesus or not. In Satan's war against Christ, he would use his followers (his offspring) to attack those of Christ.

And who is a follower of Satan? It's anyone who does not love and trust in Jesus. Those not for Christ are against Him. The natural inclination of humanity after the sin of Adam and Eve was to believe they were god rather than that the LORD Jesus is God. So they were opposed to the LORD. They wanted to join Satan's war against Christ. And all those who loved and trusted in the LORD Jesus were a target in that war. In the Garden of Eden the followers of Christ were warned that they would come under attack by Satan and his followers, as Satan sought to bring down Christ.

Abel's sacrifice

We can be certain that Adam and Eve passed onto Abel all this teaching about the gospel of Christ, testifying to their faith in the Seed[3], and also recalling how the LORD God had made an animal sacrifice in the Garden of Eden to cover their nakedness and shame. They would have remembered the awful moment of seeing the blood of a dead animal; yet at the same time being filled with joy as the LORD visually demonstrated to them how the Seed would be sacrificed so that they with all their sin could relate to holy God Most High.[4]

---

3   Their hope in the eternal life to be secured by the Sacrifice of the Seed is demonstrated by Adam naming his wife 'the mother of all the living' (Genesis 3: 20). Eve was so keen for the Saviour to come that she appeared to believe (incorrectly) that her first born son was the Seed of the Woman. When Cain was born, Eve said, 'With the help of the Lord I have brought forth a man' (Genesis 4: 2) or, as the verse could be interpreted, 'I have brought forth the LORD-man'.

4   Genesis 3: 21

The approach of fallen humanity to the holy God Almighty has 'always been through blood, and the same blood – the blood of "the Lamb slain from the foundation of the world" (Rev 13:8)'.[5]

Hearing the gospel, and filled with the Spirit, Abel showed his faith in Christ in the offering he brought to the LORD.

> Now Abel kept flocks, and Cain worked the soil. In the course of time Cain brought some of the fruits of the soil as an offering to the LORD. But Abel also brought an offering – fat portions from some of the firstborn of his flock. The LORD looked with favour on Abel and his offering, but on Cain and his offering he did not look with favour. So Cain was very angry, and his face was downcast. Then the LORD said to Cain, 'Why are you angry? Why is your face downcast? If you do what is right, will you not be accepted? But if you do not do what is right, sin is crouching at your door; it desires to have you, but you must rule over it.' Now Cain said to his brother Abel, 'Let's go out to the field.' While they were in the field, Cain attacked his brother Abel and killed him.
>
> Then the LORD said to Cain, 'Where is your brother Abel?' 'I don't know,' he replied. 'Am I my brother's keeper?' The Lord said, 'What have you done? Listen! Your brother's blood cries out to me from the ground. Now you are under a curse and driven from the ground, which opened its mouth to receive your brother's blood from your hand' (Genesis 4: 2-11).

It may be tempting to think that the LORD just doesn't like vegetarians. Some speculate that the reason for the LORD's

---

5   RS Candlish, *Expositions of Genesis* (Delaware: Sovereign Grace Publishers, 1972), 65.

preference for Abel over Cain is because Abel brought the best of his flock whereas Cain offered a mouldy bit of lettuce. But Genesis 3 had made clear that humanity's acceptance by God the Father is nothing to do with what we bring to Him. It's about what Christ, His Son, brings to the Father – in the form of His sacrificed body and blood.

There is no reason to think that Cain had less knowledge than Abel about the gospel of the Seed. Both brothers knew from their parents about the need for the Seed to shed blood to save humanity from sin and death.

But one brother trusted in the blood of Christ for his salvation; the other did not. Abel had slit the throat of the animal he brought as an offering. He held the knife and cut its neck, blood spurting from the wound, the life coming out of the animal and causing its death. He must have felt humbled that an innocent animal was dying; its blood on his hands. And as he saw that innocent blood he must have rejoiced in his heart that the future suffering of the Seed would secure his salvation; overwhelmed by the thought that although he deserved to die, the innocent Seed would be killed by the hands of wicked men doing the will of Satan. What love that the Father would send His Son to die for him.

Abel offered his sacrifice, Matthew Henry, the great Bible commentator, notes, 'in dependence upon the promise of a Redeemer'.[6] RS Candlish adds:

> Abel believed; and through his faith he received a justifying righteousness in the sight of God, even God's own righteousness in which he believed, – the finished and accepted righteousness of "the Seed of the woman",

---

6   Matthew Henry, *Commentary on the Whole Bible* (USA: Hendrickson, 1991), 17.

who is no other than the Son of God Himself (Rom. 1:17, and 3:21). And the sacrifice which he offered as the expression of his faith, and of his appropriation of the righteousness which is by faith, became, on that account, a sacrifice of a sweet-smelling Saviour (Gen. 8:21; Exod. 29:18)'[7].

Abel's offering did not itself please God Most High. The blood of an animal could not make him right with God. It was only the blood of the Seed – the First-Born Son of God – that could atone for humanity's sin, and enable them to relate to God. The blood of Jesus is superior to the blood brought by Abel[8]. But Abel's bloody offering signalled his faith in that blood – in the Sacrifice of God's Son. 'It was by this alone that he acknowledged himself a sinner, and professed faith in the promised Messiah'[9].

Cain, on the other hand, did not trust in the atoning blood of the promised Seed of the woman. He sought to satisfy God in his own way. He calculated that the fruits of his labour would reconcile himself to God. He had no sense of his sinful state before God; his heart had not been melted by the redeeming love of the Father through His Son. Cain proudly brought his sacrifice to God, expecting Him to be pleased with him.

Hence, 'the LORD looked with favour on Abel and his offering, but on Cain and his offering he did not look with favour' (Gen 4: 4-5). How could God accept anyone who wanted to be their own god? The Holy Spirit says, in the book of Hebrews, that through his faith in Christ, 'Abel

---

7   Candlish, op cit, 66.

8   See Hebrews 12: 24

9   Adam Clarke, [1831] *Commentary on the Bible* [online]. Available: http://www.godrules.net/library/clarke/clarkegen4.htm [2019, January]

brought God a better offering than Cain did. By faith he was commended as righteous when God spoke well of his offerings.' (Hebrews 11: 4).

Cain sheds Abel's blood

How did Cain respond to the LORD God saying that his brother's offering was better than his? We are told he became 'very angry' (Gen 4:5). Not repentant. Not angry at himself for his foolishness and sin. He did not fall at the LORD's feet begging His mercy. No, he was offended; he thought his offering was good enough; he thought he was good enough. Who is the LORD to tell him otherwise?

Cain had the same knowledge as his brother about the way of salvation through the Seed of the woman. He had seen his brother's example in bringing a bloody sacrifice. But Cain chose another way: his own way against Christ. It was disobedience not ignorance that was Cain's problem. So the LORD said to him: *'Why are you angry? Why is your face downcast? If you do what is right, will you not be accepted?'* (v6).

What a fantastic gospel offer. You can be accepted, the LORD told Cain. You know what you need to do. You need to turn and trust in the Sacrifice of Christ. Then you can be accepted by God Most High. You can have eternal life. You just need to stop wanting to be god yourself and accept Jesus as your LORD. Matthew Henry writes that the LORD was effectively telling Cain:

"If now thou do well, if thou repent of thy sin, reform thy heart and life, and bring thy sacrifice in a better manner, if thou not only do that which is good but do it well, thou shalt yet be accepted, thy sin shall be pardoned, thy

> comfort and honour restored, and all shall be well." See
> here the effect of a Mediator's interposal between God
> and man; ... See how... the gospel was preached, and
> the benefit of it here offered even to one of the chief of
> sinners.[10]

But Cain remained angry. His pride had been injured.
He could not stand the humiliation of having to receive
grace. He could not accept that God was to provide the
Sacrifice; that Cain need not do anything but offer his
thanksgiving to Him. It was too meek; too demeaning. Cain
had brought to the LORD his intelligence, his sophistication,
his creativity, his piety. Surely they would please God?
Surely He was satisfied with his religious homage?

Cain trusted in his own righteousness and was furious to
find that the LORD accepted Abel not him. Believing that his
works could gain him relationship with the true and living
God, Cain could not understand why the LORD looked with
favour on Abel. *Why does God accept him rather than me?*
He's just my younger brother. He's less clever than me; less
strong; less well-behaved; less good. How dare God
befriend him not me? Who does He think he is?

Cain was angry at the LORD that he could not have the
relationship with Him that Abel has. Yet did he also detest
his own heart? Was there a battle going on in Cain's soul?[11]
The LORD had offered him eternal life but instead Cain has
sought to please the LORD his own way – a way which had
proved inadequate. He knew all was not right with his Maker.
He did not have the peace and contentment possessed by
his brother. Abel regarded the LORD as his friend as well as
his God; yet the LORD was remote to Cain.

---

10   Henry, op cit, 17.

11   The rest of this section owes a further debt to Candlish , op cit, 71-72.

Cain sensed the superiority of his brother's relationship with his Creator. Can we hear him saying to himself, *Why don't I just admit to the LORD that I am wrong and turn to Him, trusting in the Seed for my salvation? Why do I not join my brother in finding peace with the true and living God? Why am I like the way I am? Why can I not change?*

Yet his heart was hard – and getting harder. His pride meant he could not bring himself to humble himself before the LORD. It was too simple a thing to accept that he could do nothing to earn his salvation. So his hatred for the LORD God deepened further. If possible, Cain would have murdered Him, but instead his anger latched onto Abel, the LORD's ambassador. Abel represented the LORD whom Cain loathed.

And so: 'Cain said to his brother Abel, "Let's go out to the field." While they were in the field, Cain attacked his brother Abel and killed him' (v8).

The Spirit and the Flesh

Cain and Abel were the first combatants in the war that had been prophesied in the Garden of Eve between Satan and the Seed of the woman. Families divide about all sorts of things, serious and trivial: which political party or football club they support; whether they prefer to be indoors or outdoors; what food they like; what hobbies they pursue. But nothing divides like Jesus. Those who don't follow Him will hate those who do. They may exhibit some self-control over that hatred, but it lurks in their hearts nonetheless. All too often their hatred becomes so intense it leads people to attack those in their family who follow the LORD Jesus.[12]

---

12   When the LORD Jesus became incarnate, He warned of the division that He creates among families: 'father against son and son against father, mother against daughter and daughter against mother… ' See Luke 12: 49-53.

And this is what we see in Cain's treatment of Abel: the brother born of the flesh persecuting the brother born of the Spirit[13].

> The spirit of the wicked one in his followers impels them to afflict and destroy all those who are partakers of the Spirit of God. Every persecutor is a legitimate son of the old murderer. This is the first triumph of Satan; it is not merely a death that he has introduced, but a violent one, as the first-fruits of sin. It is not the death of an ordinary person, but of the most holy man then in being; it is not brought about by the providence of God, or by a gradual failure and destruction of the earthly fabric, but by a violent separation of body and soul; it is not done by a common enemy, from whom nothing better could be expected, but by the hand of a brother, and for no other reason but because the object of his envy was more righteous than himself [14].

Cain's murder of Abel was an act of the flesh. But his flesh was no different from Abel's (or ours). Both Cain and Abel were children of Adam – fallen Adam. Abel's heart was as unclean as his brother's. Both persecutor and persecuted are human sinners. The difference between Abel and Cain was Jesus. Abel knew he was a sinner and sought salvation in Christ's blood in order to hide in *His* righteousness. Cain sought his own righteousness apart from Jesus and lapsed further into sin by shedding the blood of one of His followers.

It is not for us to judge the persecutor; for we share the same humanity which wars against Christ and His people. The difference between the persecutor and the persecuted

---

13   See Galatians 4: 29 which refers to another story of sibling persecution: Ishmael attacking Isaac.

14   Clarke, op cit.

is the grace of God. If we judge others, we must judge ourselves. Far better that we pray that the persecutor should come to accept the grace that we have been given. And pray that our hearts are guarded from the very self-righteousness from which we have been saved.[15]

Candlish puts all this in the following moving words:

Beware, O my soul, of the great sin of Cain. If thy heart is not right with God, thou wilt assuredly be tempted to hate and harass the godly. The spirit of ungodliness is essentially the spirit of murder. It would if it were possible, annihilate God, – for He troubles it. The next best expedient is to annihilate all on the earth that reflects His image, and testifies of Him. Hence hard thoughts of the truly righteous – suspicions – cruel surmises – evil speaking of their good and exaggeration of their evil – temptations offered to their principles – a silencing and suppressing of their testimony – violence against their persons... Let me carefully examine myself. Do I feel any pleasure when the godly man stumbles?

If so, let me be awakened in time. Let me be convinced that my real quarrel is not with him, but with his religion and his God... Then let me end this controversy at once. Let me take the offered Saviour as my own. He is mine, if I will but have Him to be mine; – mine without money

---

15 The apostle Paul testifies so powerfully to the grace of God because he never forgot that before he turned to Christ (and was on the receiving end of persecution) he had himself persecuted God's people: 'Even though I was once a blasphemer and a persecutor and a violent man, I was shown mercy because I acted in ignorance and unbelief. The grace of our Lord was poured out on me abundantly, along with the faith and love that are in Christ Jesus. Here is a trustworthy saying that deserves full acceptance: Christ Jesus came into the world to save sinners – of whom I am the worst. But for that very reason I was shown mercy so that in me, the worst of sinners, Christ Jesus might display his immense patience as an example for those who would believe in him and receive eternal life... ' (1 Timothy 1: 13-16)

and without price. I may at once, however unworthy and sinful, with all my guilt on my head, whatever that guilt may be, – ... just as I am, appropriate His sacrifice and avail myself of all its efficacy... Let me no longer resist His Spirit; ...let me submit to His righteousness, and receive remission, in the only way in which it can be bestowed, through the shedding of blood. Then, instead of seeking to brave out my continuance in sin by means of anger or sullen discontent, I may meekly and resolutely face the struggle against it and enter into the victory over it which my Lord has won.

And once we have accepted Christ as Saviour, what then?

Thus shall I taste true blessedness and peace. Yes, even though, instead of any longer persecuting the righteous, I should now be myself persecuted as Abel was. Remembering my own past feelings, I may well expect to be so, and I may well take it patiently; – especially in the view of joining the glorious company in which Abel was the first to be enrolled. Arrayed in white robes, and having come out of great tribulation, and washed their robes and made them white in the blood of the Lamb, – they are before the throne of God and serve Him day and night in His temple: and He that sitteth on the throne shall dwell among them; God shall wipe away all tears from their eyes" (Rev. 7:13-17).[16]

Not Forgotten

Cain sought to relate to God without Jesus; he rejected Jesus and that in turn drove him to attack someone who loved Jesus. Cain's sin is typical of all persecution.

But what about Abel? Martyred for the sake of Christ.

16   Candlish, op cit, 72-73

Was that it? Was his murder of any consequence to the LORD whom he served?

The LORD did not ignore what had happened; He sought out Cain to confront him about the terrible thing he had done:

> Then the LORD said to Cain, 'Where is your brother Abel?' 'I don't know,' he replied. 'Am I my brother's keeper?' The Lord said, 'What have you done? Listen! Your brother's blood cries out to me from the ground. Now you are under a curse and driven from the ground, which opened its mouth to receive your brother's blood from your hand. When you work the ground, it will no longer yield its crops for you. You will be a restless wanderer on the earth.'

> Cain said to the LORD, 'My punishment is more than I can bear. Today you are driving me from the land, and I will be hidden from your presence; I will be a restless wanderer on the earth, and whoever finds me will kill me.'

> But the LORD said to him, 'Not so; anyone who kills Cain will suffer vengeance seven times over.' Then the LORD put a mark on Cain so that no one who found him would kill him. So Cain went out from the LORD's presence and lived in the land of Nod, east of Eden. (Genesis 4: 9-16).

The LORD made clear that the murder of Abel was an offence not just against Abel but against *Him*. The LORD Jesus was His Bride's keeper. A follower of the LORD is one with Him – and so to persecute Abel was to persecute the LORD. His servant's blood cried out to Him from the ground. His creation had been defiled; polluted by death. The earth was designed for life; it could not cope with death. It was appalled by blood. It rejected the one whose hand had caused it to be spilled.

Cain's crime was not unnoticed by the LORD; it would not go unpunished. There would be justice. Cain escaped the immediate penalty of death for his act of murder but was cursed for his evil deeds. He was forced away from the presence of the LORD to wander in the wilderness; the LORD placing a mark on him to protect him from being killed. Did Cain use that opportunity to repent of his sins and accept the bloody sacrifice of the LORD Jesus? Did he find rest in the LORD or did he wander through the world for the rest of the life without finding peace? It seems he chose the latter course. The LORD put His mark upon Cain to protect him from immediate judgement but also to remind humanity of the exile which results from rejecting the true and living God and persecuting His people.

Cain's name lives on today, but only as an example to avoid. It is not just in the book of Genesis that the Holy Spirit teaches us about Cain; elsewhere in the Scriptures we are warned to be on guard against those who like Cain reject the grace of God and deny the LORD Jesus:

> Dear friends, although I was very eager to write to you about the salvation we share, I felt compelled to write and urge you to contend for the faith that was once for all entrusted to God's holy people. For certain individuals whose condemnation was written about long ago have secretly slipped in among you. They are ungodly people, who pervert the grace of our God into a license for immorality and deny Jesus Christ our only Sovereign and Lord... Woe to them! They have taken the way of Cain. (Jude vv3-4,11)

And lest we become proud, we must guard our own hearts against the hatred that sinners have:

> For this is the message you heard from the beginning: we should love one another. Do not be like Cain, who belonged to the evil one and murdered his brother. And why did he murder him? Because his own actions were evil and his brother's were righteous. Do not be surprised, my brothers and sisters if the world hates you. We know that we have passed from death to life, because we love each other. Anyone who does not love remains in death. Anyone who hates a brother or sister is a murderer, and you know that no murderer has eternal life residing in him. (1 John 3:11-15).

Note the irony. It was Cain who murdered Abel and yet it was Cain who lost his life not Abel. It is Cain who is cut off from life with the true and living God; who loses his soul.

There will be a reckoning for the blood of Abel and all those who have been persecuted:

> Woe to you, teachers of the law and Pharisees, you hypocrites! You build tombs for the prophets and decorate the graves of the righteous. And you say, 'If we had lived in the days of our ancestors, we would not have taken part with them in shedding the blood of the prophets.' So you testify against yourselves that you are the descendants of those who murdered the prophets. Go ahead, then, and complete what your ancestors started!
>
> You snakes! You brood of vipers! How will you escape being condemned to hell? Therefore I am sending you prophets and sages and teachers. Some of them you will kill and crucify; others you will flog in your synagogues and pursue from town to town. And so upon you will

come all the righteous blood that has been shed on earth, from the blood of righteous Abel to the blood of Zechariah son of Berekiah, whom you murdered between the temple and the altar. Truly I tell you, all this will come on this generation (Matthew 23: 29-36).

The blood of the persecuted is not forgotten by the LORD. It continues to cry out to Him, until the time of final judgement of the universe when their blood will be wiped from the earth and their persecutors will be banished forever from His world. Unlike his brother, Abel's memory is cherished; his soul is safe in the LORD's bosom as he waits for the Day of Resurrection. Abel was persecuted by his brother for the sake of the LORD Jesus Christ. And the LORD remembers his blood. Abel's faith in Christ 'still speaks, even though he is dead' (Hebrews 11: 4).

Are you being persecuted by Cain? Is a member of your family attacking you because of Jesus? It's painful; intensely painful. Is there any escape? Will it end? Who can take this pain away? Does the Triune God care? Has He forgotten me? Is He hearing my prayers?

The story of Abel teaches us that God the Father, Son and Holy Spirit always notices what's happening to His people; He shares the pain they share; He never forgets the suffering of His people; He will bring justice on those who attack; and He remains close to His people always.

CHAPTER TWO

PERSECUTION OF THE CHURCH

As Abel was attacked by his brother, so any follower of the LORD Jesus may experience persecution by a member of their family. But at particular times in particular places the whole Church may come under attack by those hostile to the LORD Jesus. Political and religious authorities may regard the followers of Christ as a threat and be moved to destroy their property; burn their villages; take away the men and shoot them; rape the women; abduct their children. Or murder every one of them.

It's not just one person who suffers; an attempt is made to eliminate hundreds, thousands, even millions of Christ's disciples.

The book of Exodus tells how the Church faced such persecution when living in the land of Egypt. Yet Pharaoh's attempt to destroy the Church was not successful. The Passover and the Exodus are unique ways by which the Church escaped from its suffering; yet are recorded in the Scriptures so that the followers of Christ in all generations may have confidence in the LORD Jesus' power and victory over the enemies of His Church.

The events are covered in Exodus chapters 1 to 15 and the focus of this study is on the first three chapters of that book.

The Growth of the Church

Many years after the time of Cain and Abel, the LORD Jesus was sent by the LORD of heaven to call Abraham to Himself. God the Father, Son and Holy Spirit promised Abraham that he would be the ancestor of the Seed ('who is Christ'[1]) – the Seed of the Women who was to crush the devil and purchase eternal life for all those who trusted in Him. And Abraham was told that, because of his link to Christ, he would be made 'into a great nation' and 'all peoples on earth' would be blessed through him. Over time, the gospel of Christ was to spread through the whole world building up the body of God's people which would be as numerous as the stars in the sky[2].

This great nation of God's people – which was to become known as the nation of Israel – was founded through Abraham and his natural children but was for all those with faith in Christ. Not all of Abraham's natural children were followers of the LORD Jesus; and one did not have to be a natural child of Abraham to be a follower of Christ. 'If you belong to Christ, then you are Abraham's seed'[3]. A true child of Abraham trusted in Christ and His Father, and possessed the Holy Spirit.[4]

The LORD God promised that this great nation of all peoples had a glorious future. The land – the whole world – would be given to the Seed and all who trusted in Him.[5] They would live forever in the creation – the creation made new by the suffering and glory of Christ. As a sign of this

1   Galatians 3: 16

2   Genesis 12: 1-7, 13: 6, 15: 5, Galatians 3: 8.

3   Galatians 3: 29

4   Deuteronomy 30: 29; Romans 2: 28-29

5   Genesis 12: 7; 13: 15

promise, the LORD foretold that Abraham's descendants would take possession of a land – the land of Canaan.

These were fantastic gospel promises. Yet, the LORD warned Abraham, by being linked to Christ, he and his descendants must expect persecution. Persecution had not died out with the murder of Abel. The LORD Jesus divided nations and families. The LORD told Abraham: 'I will bless those who bless you, and *whoever curses you* I will curse' (Genesis 12: 3). Abraham and his descendants – the nation of Israel – were so intimately connected to Christ that they would suffer as He would suffer, and when they suffered He suffered. In the midst of the promises the LORD made to Abraham about the Seed and the new creation, He made a specific prophecy about the persecution of Israel:

> The LORD said to [Abraham], 'Know for certain that for four hundred years your descendants will be strangers in a country not their own and that they will be enslaved and ill-treated there. But I will punish the nation they serve as slaves, and afterwards they will come out with great possessions.' (Genesis 15: 13-14)

Enslaving the Church

Many years later, after the death of Abraham, this prophecy began to be fulfilled. The great grandson of Abraham, Joseph, was exiled from Canaan to Egypt. The rest of Joseph's family followed him to Egypt to escape the famine in the land – a missionary band of 70 sent amongst the nations.[6]

6   See Genesis 46, and Psalm 105: 16-23. Joseph's life (recorded in Genesis 37-50) was a witness to the Promised Seed. He was betrayed by his brothers for a few silver coins; unjustly condemned as a criminal although an innocent man; yet ended up as a ruler of the nations – a man under authority, fulfilling God's will to save His people. Glory followed suffering.

At that time, Egypt and its leader were happy to have Abraham's children live among them. They brought the blessings of Christ to them. They saw the way that the true and living God acted through Joseph. The Pharaoh recognised that it was an honour to have this small nation in his land because of its relation to Christ, the Saviour of the world. Israel – Jacob, the grandson of Abraham – had also received the promise of being an ancestor of the LORD Jesus. And so even though he was ruler of a great nation, Pharaoh sought the blessing of Israel[7], and took care of the Seed-bearing nation which had been entrusted to his keeping.

Yet things were going to change:

Now Joseph and all his brothers and all that generation died, but the Israelites were exceedingly fruitful; they multiplied greatly, increased in numbers and became so numerous that the land was filled with them. Then a new king, to whom Joseph meant nothing, came to power in Egypt. "Look," he said to his people, "the Israelites have become far too numerous for us. Come, we must deal shrewdly with them or they will become even more numerous and, if war breaks out, will join our enemies, fight against us and leave the country." (Exodus 1: 6-10)

When Egypt's new king looked at the nation of Israel, he did not rejoice in their witness to the LORD Jesus. He did not see that they were the people from whom the Promised Seed would be born; the people through whom the true and living God was acting in history to bring about the salvation of the whole world. The king saw instead a political threat. This Pharaoh had no concern for anything other than his

---

7   Genesis 28: 10-15; 47: 7-10.

own temporal power. His eyes were closed to spiritual reality. To him, Israel was not a blessing to the nations, but a problem to solve. The Israelites had multiplied into a vast nation which was still growing – through natural growth, and through the conversion of Egyptians (and other peoples) to the LORD Jesus.[8]

Given the concern of Egypt's king to maintain his own power, it was entirely natural that he should regard Israel as a danger. However useful to the economy, the Israelites were not *real* Egyptians. Their duty to Pharaoh and Egypt was weak. They claimed that the LORD was their King. One can imagine the king's line of thinking. *Well, they could believe whatever religious nonsense they like – but a true Egyptian swears loyalty to me. Anyone who doesn't do that cannot be trusted. Anyone not for us must be against us. If war breaks out, they are likely to go over to the other side. They are the enemy within.*

Focused only on practical politics, Egypt's ruler sought to 'deal shrewdly' with the Israelites. He came up with a simple strategy to address the political problem they represented – he ordered his people to put the Israelites into slavery:

> So they put slave masters over them to oppress them with forced labour, and they built Pithom and Rameses as store cities for Pharaoh. But the more they were oppressed, the more they multiplied and spread; so the Egyptians came to dread the Israelites and worked them ruthlessly. They made their lives bitter with harsh labour in brick and mortar and with all kinds of work in the fields; in all their harsh labour the Egyptians worked them ruthlessly. (Exodus 1: 11-14)

8   See Leviticus 24: 10

Blind as he was to spiritual reality, the king could not see that it was the true and living God who was making Israel fruitful. So he adopted an even more draconian approach to try and deal with his enemy:

> The king of Egypt said to the Hebrew midwives, whose names were Shiprah and Puah, "When you are helping the Hebrew women during childbirth on the delivery stool, if you see that the baby is a boy, kill him; but if it is a girl, let her live." (Exodus 1: 15-16)

Obsessed by the need to maintain his power, the king sought to control the growth of Israel by authorising infanticide. He seemed to hope to eliminate the nation entirely over time. And if he did he would put at risk the arrival of the Promised Seed who was to come from Israel. This was the work of Satan.

Facing up to Pharaoh

So how were the midwives to respond to this persecution of the Church? Should they rise up with their fellow Israelites and overthrow the king? Or should they put their trust in him and become Egyptians? Should their allegiance be such that they were prepared to do anything that he asked?

Terrible though the king's request was, the midwives must have been tempted to obey it in order to keep their own lives. 'The midwives, however, feared God... ' (v17).

The allegiance of the midwives was to the LORD their God, not this dictator. Their faith was in Christ, the Promised Seed, who was to conquer sin and death. Trusting in the LORD Jesus, 'righteousness had been credited to them' (Genesis 15: 6). They were filled with the Holy Spirit and sought to live for their Saviour. They were prepared to put up with the trials of this life because, like Abraham,

Isaac and Jacob, 'they were longing for a better country' (Hebrews 11: 16). They could take confidence from the prophecy of Enoch that, whatever the suffering they endured at the hand of the king, the LORD Jesus would come one day and judge the living and the dead:

> See, the Lord is coming with thousands upon thousands of his holy ones to judge everyone, and to convict all of them of all the ungodly acts they have committed in their ungodliness, and of all the defiant words ungodly sinners have spoken against him. (Jude 14-15)

The Hebrew midwives were prepared to obey Egypt's king; yet not because of his greatness: no, because they feared the LORD. There was never a choice between the king and *the* King. The *LORD Jesus is* the King. The women's allegiance was always to Him; they obeyed the king only because they obeyed *the* King. *He* had placed them in Egypt and they served Him by respecting the king of the land in which the Church resided, however hard he made the Israelites work.

The midwives were prepared to put up with much. But they could not kill members of the LORD's people. To obey the King, they *had* to disobey the king, even if that meant they themselves would be killed. Matthew Henry comments:

> If men's commands be any way contrary to the commands of God, we must obey God and not man (Acts 4, 19; 29). No power on earth can warrant us, much less oblige us, to sin against God, our chief Lord. Again, where the fear of God rules in the heart, it will preserve it from the snare which the inordinate fear of man brings.[9]

9   Henry, op cit, 96

The midwives could not deny their LORD and Saviour. And so they 'did not do what the king of Egypt had told them to do; they let the boys live' (Exodus 1: 17)

Naturally the king was furious.

> He summoned the midwives and asked them, "Why have you done this? Why have you let the boys live?" The midwives answered Pharaoh, "Hebrew women are not like Egyptian women; they are vigorous and give birth before the midwives arrive." So God was kind to the midwives and the people increased and became even more numerous. And because the midwives feared God, he gave them families of their own. (Exodus 1: 18-21)

It may seem that the midwives' response verged on the disingenuous but Matthew Henry comments as follows:

> I see no reason we have to doubt the truth of this; it is plain that the Hebrews were now under an extraordinary blessing of increase, which may well be supposed to have this effect, that the women had very quick and easy labour, and, the mothers and children being both lively, they seldom needed the help of midwives: this these midwives took notice of, and, concluding it to be the finger of God, were thereby emboldened to disobey the king, in favour of those whom Heaven thus favoured, and with this justified themselves before Pharaoh, when he called them to an account for it... Note, God is a readier help to his people in distress than any other helpers are, and often anticipates them with the blessings of his goodness; such deliverances lay them under peculiarly strong obligations.[10]

---

10   Ibid, 96.

And so the LORD blessed the midwives, because in the face of the Church's persecution they feared Him and not Pharaoh – because they were kind to His people, which He took as kindness to Himself. Yet the king's madness raged even greater:

> Then Pharaoh gave this order to all his people: "Every Hebrew boy that is born you must throw into the Nile, but let every girl live"' (Exodus 1: 22).

The Triune God rules

In the splendour of the royal palace, surrounded by yes men, the Pharaoh must have believed he controlled the whole world. If he said this, it happened; if he ordered that, it became law; if he wanted anything; he got it.

That the king's violent actions against the Israelites did not seem to be effective only fuelled his murderous rage. *I am the Ruler of the universe. My will must be done.*

> In his pride the wicked man does not seek [the LORD];
>   in all his thoughts there is no room for God...
> He says to himself, "Nothing will ever shake me."
>   He swears, "No one will ever do me harm."
> His mouth is full of lies and threats;
>   trouble and evil are under his tongue...
> His victims are crushed, they collapse;
>   they fall under his strength.
> He says to himself, "God will never notice;
>   he covers his face and never sees."...
> Why does the wicked man revile God?
>   Why does he say to himself,
>   "He won't call me to account"?
> But you, God, see the trouble of the afflicted;
>   you consider their grief and take it in hand.
> (Psalm 10: 4, 6-7, 10-11, 13-14)

The king could not see how his actions operated in relation to the Three Persons of God who controls the world. The king sought to persecute the Church; the Triune God blessed it with greater growth. The ruler spluttered and raged; the true and living God laughed at his impotence. The king ordered all Israelite baby boys to be thrown in the Nile; and then the LORD saved one of them and had him brought up under Pharaoh's nose in his own palace!

This baby boy was Moses – 'no ordinary child'[11] – so full of the Spirit his leadership qualities were evident from birth. The LORD oversaw his rescue from the Egyptians in such a way that he was taken into the royal palace by Pharaoh's daughter and nursed by his mother there.

As Moses grew up in Pharaoh's palace, he must have been tempted, as an adopted Egyptian, to turn his back on his LORD Jesus and His people. He must have been tempted to become an Egyptian – to put his faith in Pharaoh and his gods, and to carry on enjoying the riches and privilege he had experienced in his youth. Why give them up and endure the sufferings which the Israelites were enduring? The Holy Spirit tells us the answer:

> By faith Moses, when he had grown up, refused to be known as the son of Pharaoh's daughter. He chose to be mistreated along with the people of God rather than to enjoy the fleeting pleasures of sin. **He regarded disgrace for the sake of Christ as of greater value than the treasures of Egypt, because he was looking ahead to his reward.** By faith he left Egypt, not fearing the king's anger... ' (Hebrews 11: 24-27).

11   Exodus 2: 1-4. Acts 7: 20; Hebrews 11: 23.

Moses was prepared to give up his life of privilege 'for the sake of Christ'. The LORD Jesus, not Pharaoh, was his God. The people of Israel had no option but to endure persecution. Moses *chose* to join them in their suffering. He left behind the palace of a pagan king because he wanted to be part of the Church[12] of the living God and to serve Him. He trusted in the Promised Seed for his salvation. The riches of fellowship with God the Father, Son and Holy Spirit far outweighed anything Pharaoh could give him. Moses chose to suffer with the people of God – to share in the sufferings of the Promised Seed; to face disgrace 'for the sake of Christ'.

Pharaoh exerted all his power to persecute the Israelites; yet failed to realise that he had brought up the future leader of the Church in his own palace. Everything the king did was within God's sovereign will. His life had been given to him by the LORD; and soon enough the LORD took it away again. The king died (Ex 2: 23). The Pharaoh who had ordained the murder of the Israelite boys went the way of all flesh; one minute he was powerful and wealthy; then his body lay in the ground; he returned to the dust, his soul alienated from the true and living God.

The Rescuer comes down

The king of Egypt may have died but Israel remained in slavery. A new Pharaoh took over who shared his predecessor's hatred of the Church and its witness to the LORD Jesus. But the time was coming for the true and living God to act and fulfil the promise He had made to Abraham:

12   Acts 7: 38 refers to Israel as the 'assembly' or 'congregation' or 'church'.

> The Israelites groaned in their slavery and cried out, and their cry for help because of their slavery went up to God. God heard their groaning and he remembered his covenant with Abraham, with Isaac and with Jacob. So God looked on the Israelites and was concerned about them. (Exodus 2: 23-25)

The suffering of His people grieved the Triune God. He shared their agony. And He acted in response. God the Father sent His Angel – the visible Person of God – the pre-incarnate LORD Jesus Christ. God the Father sent His Angel to save His people. The Angel met Moses to commission him to lead God's people:

> Now Moses was tending the flock of Jethro his father-in-law, the priest of Midian, and he led the flock to the far side of the wilderness and came to Horeb, the mountain of God. There the angel of the Lord appeared to him in flames of fire from within a bush. Moses saw that though the bush was on fire it did not burn up. So Moses thought, 'I will go over and see this strange sight – why the bush does not burn up.'
>
> When the Lord saw that he had gone over to look, God called to him from within the bush, 'Moses! Moses!' (Exodus 3: 1-4)

Moses was given a tremendous visible sign of the gospel of the Promised Seed in which the Angel of the LORD stood in the fire of God, reminding Moses that He was to suffer for His people – that when He came in human flesh, He would stand in the fire of the Triune God's wrath for them. God the Father so loved the world that He was prepared to give up His First-Born Son to save it. The First-Born so loved His Bride that He was prepared to lay down His life for Her.

In the fire of God which burnt in the bush, the Angel of the LORD demonstrated to Moses that He would save His people from their sins; He would give them life beyond death; there would be resurrection. He was and is the God of eternal life: He was, the Angel said to Moses, 'the God of Abraham, Isaac and Jacob'.[13] The patriarchs had died a long time ago but they lived on in everlasting relationship with the LORD; dwelling in Paradise, waiting for Resurrection Day. All those who trusted in the Angel of the LORD had eternal life.

Having reminded Moses of the eternal salvation of His people, the Angel of the LORD promised a more immediate rescue, which would typify His eternal work of salvation:

> The LORD said, "I have indeed seen the misery of my people in Egypt. I have heard them crying out because of their slave drivers, and I am concerned about their suffering. So I have come down to rescue them from the hand of the Egyptians and to bring them up out of that land into a good and spacious land, a land flowing with milk and honey—the home of the Canaanites, Hittites, Amorites, Perizzites, Hivites and Jebusites. And now the cry of the Israelites has reached me, and I have seen the way the Egyptians are oppressing them. So now, go. I am sending you to Pharaoh to bring my people the Israelites out of Egypt." (Exodus 3: 7-10)

The rescue plan was as follows:

> You and the elders [of Israel] are to go to the king of Egypt and say to him, the LORD, the God of the Hebrews, has met with us. Let us take a three-day journey into the

---

13   See Exodus 3: 1-6; Matthew 22: 23-33.

wilderness to offer sacrifices to the Lord our God." But I know that the king of Egypt will not let you go unless a mighty hand compels him. So I will stretch out my hand and strike the Egyptians with all the wonders that I will perform among them. After that, he will let you go.

And I will make the Egyptians favourably disposed towards this people, so that when you leave you will not go empty-handed. Every woman is to ask her neighbour and any woman living in her house for articles of silver and gold and for clothing, which you will put on your sons and daughters. And so you will plunder the Egyptians.' (Exodus 3: 18-22)

Pharaoh defeated

All these prophecies uttered by the Angel of the LORD were fulfilled. The Pharaoh did not heed Moses' request to let God's people leave Egypt. He wanted to keep the Israelites as slaves. The fact that the LORD was asking him to release His people through Moses meant nothing to him. 'Who is the LORD, that I should obey him and let Israel go? I do not know the LORD and I will not let Israel go.' (Exodus 5: 2).

Even when Moses warned Pharaoh what would happen to him and the Egyptians – that the LORD was to send plagues upon the land – he did not listen. He could have repented, turned to the LORD Jesus and joined His Church. Yet he hardened his heart; and took out his anger on the Israelites, working them to the bone, making their lives more and more difficult.[14]

Moses, full of faith in Christ, bravely confronted Pharaoh, speaking the words of the LORD to him. Moses faced death

14   Exodus 5: 4-18.

every time he entered the palace – the palace where he had once lived in splendour. But he trusted in His LORD and Saviour. Moses trusted his life to the One who could walk through the fire of the Triune God's wrath – he feared the LORD not Pharaoh. Moses knew that his LORD would enable him to stand before the king; he knew that his LORD would overcome Pharaoh. With the LORD Jesus on his side, Moses had no need to be scared of the king.

It was Pharaoh who should have been scared. But he paid no attention to the Word of the LORD proclaimed by Moses. He showed some acknowledgement of the LORD's power when a plague came upon the Egyptians; then when it passed, he felt strong enough to ignore the LORD. 'When Pharaoh saw that there was relief, he hardened his heart and would not listen to Moses, just as the LORD had said' (Exodus 8: 15).

Like his predecessor, the Pharaoh thought he could treat God's people how he wished; that he could do what he liked without accountability to anyone. But the Triune God remained in control. The LORD had foretold in Exodus 3 that Pharaoh wouldn't listen to Moses; that the king would harden his heart to Him. And He warned that it would come to the point when 'I will harden his heart so that he will not let the people go (4: 21). The LORD would hand over the ruler to his selfish desires – to his will to be his own god. The king would become incapable of obeying the LORD.

Pharaoh thought he was defying God; that he was in charge of his own destiny; but in reality he was merely fulfilling the LORD's plans. Pharaoh's power was given to him only to show how weak he was compared to the LORD. The king was allowed to commit his wicked deeds only to demonstrate how the Triune God would overcome evil. The LORD had told him that very truth through Moses:

> 'I have raised you up for this very purpose, that I might show you my power and that my name might be proclaimed in all the earth' (Exodus 9: 16).

The LORD Jesus made clear that His confrontation with Pharaoh was set up by the Triune God not just so He could rescue His people from Egypt but in order that He could display to the whole world His eternal plan of salvation. He was going to show His power such that His Name would be famous in all the earth. What power? The gospel of Christ. That is the power of God. That is the power which was going to destroy Pharaoh's power.

It may have appeared that Pharaoh dictated what happened in Egypt; that he could treat people in any way he wanted. Even the followers of the Triune God might have been tempted to despair: *Where are you God? Don't you care? Why don't You do something about this evil? Why do the wicked get away with their crimes?*

But through the plagues sent on Egypt, the Triune God revealed Himself with devastating authority; redisplaying the power He had shown in creation; separating light and dark; demonstrating His division between good and evil; and making a clear distinction between His people and those of Pharaoh[15]. It culminated in the day of the Passover when the Angel of the LORD was sent by the LORD in heaven to destroy the power of Egypt: to overturn its wickedness and to condemn its gods[16]. The Angel of the LORD was sent through Egypt to put to death all the first-

---

15   Exodus 8: 23, 9: 4, 11: 7.

16   Exodus 12: 12

born in the land – Egyptian or Israelite. All were condemned to die but the Angel of the LORD passed over the homes of anyone – Egyptian or Israelite – who placed the blood of a lamb on their doorway. The lamb died instead of them. Anyone could be saved if they trusted in the blood of the lamb – if they had faith in the blood of the Passover Lamb.[17]

Freedom

The Passover shattered the power of Pharaoh, redeeming Israel from its slavery. As noted earlier, the might of Pharaoh only served to demonstrate the true power of the gospel of Christ, revealed in the blood of the Passover Lamb. The power of God overcame the power of Pharaoh. The Lamb suffered in order to release the Church from its suffering.

Free from its captivity, Israel (comprising those naturally born into it and the foreigners who had joined it) travelled to the Promised Land. Pharaoh and his horsemen chased after them but the Israelites could not be recaptured. The Angel of God divided the waters of the Red Sea so that the Israelites escaped on dry ground; then He stood between the armies of Egypt and Israel, bringing light to the latter, darkness to the former. As Israel made it to the other side of the sea, the LORD Jesus brought back the waters destroying the Egyptians. The persecutors of His people were dead and all the world could see that the LORD had gained 'glory through Pharaoh and all his army, through his chariots and his horsemen'[18].

And so the LORD Jesus 'delivered His people out of Egypt' (Jude 5); He redeemed His people out from slavery

---

17   Exodus 12 (note how the LORD makes room for those who were not natural born Israelites to take part in the Passover in verses 48-49).

18   Exodus 14: 17 – see whole chapter.

so that they might have fellowship with God the Father, Son and Spirit, and enter the Promised Land, taking with them the goods of the Egyptians[19]. The LORD Jesus took His people into 'the land of milk and honey' – the land of Canaan that served as a sign of the new creation.

As Jonathan Edwards, the great 18th century theologian, comments:

> The people of Israel went out with a high hand, and Christ went before them in a pillar of cloud and fire. There was a glorious triumph over earth and hell in that deliverance. When Pharaoh and his hosts, and Satan by them, pursued the people, Christ overthrew them in the Red sea; the Lord triumphed gloriously; the horse and his rider he cast into the sea, and there they slept their sleep, and never followed the children of Israel any more.

> ...Thus Christ, the angel of God's presence, in his love and his pity, redeemed his people, and carried them in the days of old as on eagles' wings, so that none of their proud and spiteful enemies, neither Egyptians nor devils, could touch them.[20]

Remembering Israel's Salvation

Through the Passover and Exodus, the LORD Jesus not only defeated the power of Pharaoh; He gave a dramatic sign that He would defeat all the evil in the universe. He was going to redeem His people from their slavery to the gods of the world. But at what cost! It was to take the sacrifice of

---

19   Exodus 12: 31-36

20   Jonathan Edwards, [1774] *A History of the Work of Redemption* [Online] Available: http://www.ccel.org/ccel/edwards/works1.xii.iv.iv.html [2019, January]

the Lamb – the death of the Son of God – in order to save His Bride and defeat the evil of those who attack Her.

Little wonder, therefore, that God the Father, Son and Holy Spirit made sure that His Church – and the whole world – would never forget the Passover and Exodus. Even before the Passover happened, the LORD gave His people instructions on how to commemorate it.[21] And after Israel had escaped from the clutches of Pharaoh and his army, Moses sang praise to the Angel of the LORD for His victory and the triumph of the Church over their enemies:

The LORD is my strength and my defence;
    he has become my salvation.
…Your right hand, LORD,
    shattered the enemy.
In the greatness of your majesty
    you threw down those who opposed you.
    …The enemy boasted,
    'I will pursue, I will overtake them.
I will divide the spoils;
    I will gorge myself on them.
I will draw my sword
    and my hand will destroy them.'
But you blew with your breath,
    and the sea covered them.
    …Who among the gods
is like you, LORD?
Who is like you—
    majestic in holiness,
awesome in glory,
    working wonders?
You stretch out your right hand,
    and the earth swallows your enemies.
(Exodus 15: 2, 6-7, 9-12)

21   Exodus 12: 1-20

When the Church is facing persecution for the sake of Christ, the Holy Spirit reminds us of the LORD's mighty power in rescuing Israel from Egypt. Looking back to the Passover and Exodus gives the Church in all generations confidence in the LORD Jesus:[22]

> I cried out to God for help;
>> I cried out to God to hear me.
> When I was in distress, I sought the Lord;
>> at night I stretched out untiring hands,
>> and I would not be comforted.
>
> ...I remembered my songs in the night.
>> My heart meditated and my spirit asked:
>
> "Will the Lord reject forever?
>> Will he never show his favour again?
> Has his unfailing love vanished forever?
>> Has his promise failed for all time?
> Has God forgotten to be merciful?
>> Has he in anger withheld his compassion?"
>
> Then I thought, "To this I will appeal:
>> the years when the Most High stretched out his
> right hand.
> I will remember the deeds of the Lord;
>> yes, I will remember your miracles of long ago.
> I will consider all your works
>> and meditate on all your mighty deeds."
>
> Your ways, God, are holy.
>> What god is as great as our God?

---

22   See Deuteronomy 4: 32, 34, Joshua 24, 2 Samuel 7:18, 22-24, 1 Kings 8, Nehemiah 9. Psalm 78, 105, 114, 135, 136, Micah 7, 1 Corinthians 10, Acts 7. See Joshua 2: 8-11 and 9: 7-9 for examples of the knowledge which the nations had of the LORD's work in redeeming Israel from Egypt.

You are the God who performs miracles;
    you display your power among the peoples.
With your mighty arm you redeemed your people,
    the descendants of Jacob and Joseph.

The waters saw you, God,
    the waters saw you and writhed;
    the very depths were convulsed.
The clouds poured down water,
    the heavens resounded with thunder;
    your arrows flashed back and forth.
Your thunder was heard in the whirlwind,
    your lightning lit up the world;
 the earth trembled and quaked.
Your path led through the sea,
    your way through the mighty waters,
    though your footprints were not seen.

You led your people like a flock
    by the hand of Moses and Aaron.

(Psalm 77: 1-2, 6-20)

Praise be to the God of Abraham, Isaac and Jacob, the Saviour of Israel, the Saviour of the world.

CHAPTER THREE

PERSECUTION WITHIN THE CHURCH

A Christian minister said to me some time ago that he had been on the receiving end of a lot of abuse, even violence, from the adherents of other religions. But he had experienced much deeper pain from the actions and words of his own church members.

Count Zinzendorf fearlessly led the Moravians in their evangelism across the world but he was devasted when people from within the church community abused him: their ringleaders calling him 'the Beast out of the Abyss'.[1]

How should church leaders react when they are attacked, not by those outside the church but from within? When they are slandered, bullied, shouted at? When another unpleasant note is sent to them? When their family is criticised? A faction within their congregation tries to evict them from their leadership role?

How should they deal with those causing trouble?

The Holy Spirit gives a number of examples of such 'internal persecution' in the book of Exodus, where the leaders of the Church are attacked by its members. The particular focus of this chapter is Exodus 17: 1-7.

1   Wemmer P, *Count Zinzendorf and the Spirit of the Moravians,* Xulon Press,2013, 88-93.

Grumbling in the Desert

As we saw in the previous chapter, the Church had been liberated from its slavery in Egypt through the Passover and Exodus. It was then led by the Angel of the LORD through the desert. The Angel of LORD had revealed His mighty power and love to redeem His people from Egypt, and He carried His people out of slavery on 'eagles' wings'[2]. His purpose was to lead Israel to Mount Sinai in order to meet God Most High[3]. The Church had been redeemed from their bondage by God the Son through the power of the Spirit so that they might have fellowship with God the Father.

Israel's journey to Mount Sinai took place in a number of stages:

> The whole Israelite community set out from the Desert of Sin, travelling from place to place as the Lord commanded. They camped at Rephidim, but there was no water for the people to drink. (Exodus 17: 1)

The Angel of the LORD had miraculously freed the people from slavery and had helped them cross the Red Sea out of Egypt. So surely He could meet their need for water? They just needed to call on Him; to trust in His goodness. But:

> …they quarrelled with Moses and said, 'Give us water to drink.' Moses replied, 'Why do you quarrel with me? Why do you put the Lord to the test?' But the people were thirsty for water there, and they grumbled against Moses. They said, 'Why did you bring us up out of Egypt to make us and our children and livestock die of thirst?'

---

2   Exodus 19: 4

3   Exodus 19-20

> Then Moses cried out to the Lord, 'What am I to do with these people? They are almost ready to stone me.' (Exodus 17: 2-4)

The people grumbled. Almost the minute the Israelites had escaped slavery in Egypt they had started to grumble – first about the lack of water in the Desert of Shur; then about the want of food in the Desert of Sin[4]. The LORD heard their cries and provided for them, promising them each day they would be given bread and meat:

> Moses and Aaron said to all the Israelites, 'In the evening you will know that it was the Lord who brought you out of Egypt, and in the morning you will see the glory of the Lord, because he has heard your grumbling against him. Who are we, that you should grumble against us?' Moses also said, 'You will know that it was the Lord when he gives you meat to eat in the evening and all the bread you want in the morning, because he has heard your grumbling against him. Who are we? You are not grumbling against us, but against the Lord.'

> Then Moses told Aaron, 'Say to the entire Israelite community, "Come before the Lord, for he has heard your grumbling."'

> While Aaron was speaking to the whole Israelite community, they looked towards the desert, and there was the glory of the Lord appearing in the cloud.

> The Lord said to Moses, 'I have heard the grumbling of the Israelites. Tell them, "At twilight you will eat meat, and in the morning you will be filled with bread. Then you will know that I am the Lord your God."' (Exodus 16: 6-12)

4   Exodus 15: 22-25 and chapter 16

The LORD called the Israelites to trust in Him each day and receive the food He gave them. They were to feed on Him – because He was the bread of life, sent by His Father in heaven.[5] They must look beyond their merely physical existence. They were to feed on Him and live.

Feeding and drinking on the LORD Jesus was life; He gave *and* (temporarily) withheld food and water so that they might learn about the true, everlasting life to be found in Him – food that never spoilt; living water that always satisfied. The very reason the Angel of the LORD was leading the people through the desert was 'to humble and test' them in order their hearts would be faithful to Him, for through that faith they would have eternal life[6].

Yet the people just wanted food and water: their god was their stomach; their minds were set on earthly things[7]. So even though they had seen the Angel of the LORD provide them with all they needed each day, here they were at Nephilim, grumbling again that they were thirsty. They did not see that the LORD was testing their faithfulness. Rather, they tested *His* faithfulness. Their hearts were saying: *Did He really promise to lead us safely to the Promised Land? Did He really say He would look after us? Does He really have the power to provide for us?*

'Why do you put the LORD to the test?' Moses said to them (Exodus 17: 2).

Rather than calling upon the goodness of the Triune God when in need, the people were angry with Him. Such was the irrational anger of the Israelites that they even expressed

---

5   John 5: 25-59

6   Deuteronomy 8:2, 16, Exodus 15:25, Exodus 16:4 and Psalm 81:7

7   Philippians 3: 21.

the desire to return to Egypt (17: 3). They were on a wonderful journey accompanied by the LORD Jesus to meet God the Father at Mount Sinai and then travel onto the Promised Land. Yet the Israelites yearned to return to Egypt and be ruled by a pagan king, living among the idols of Egypt. This was a recurring desire of the Israelites throughout the 40 years they spent in the desert. They had been redeemed from slavery in Egypt yet their hearts remained enslaved to sin. Time after time, Israel tested the LORD Jesus, rebelling against Him. They 'vexed the Holy One of Israel' (Psalm 78: 41).

Grumbling against Moses

The people were angry with the LORD Jesus; yet much of their anger was directed at Moses, as can be seen by looking at the Exodus 17 passage again:

> They quarrelled with <u>Moses</u> and said, 'Give us water to drink.' Moses replied, 'Why do you quarrel with <u>me</u>? Why do you put the LORD to the test?'

> But the people were thirsty for water there, and they grumbled against <u>Moses</u>. They said, 'Why did <u>you</u> bring us up out of Egypt to make us and our children and livestock die of thirst?' Then Moses cried out to the LORD, 'What am I to do with these people? They are almost ready to stone <u>me</u>.' (Exodus 17: 2-4)

Moses had confronted Pharaoh to plead for the release of the Israelites; he had brought down plagues on the Egyptians; he faithfully served the Angel of the LORD in defeating the power of Egypt and redeeming the people from their slavery. And yet now members of the Church grumbled against him. Hatred for him built up in their hearts and their hatred led to murderous thoughts against him. They wanted to stone him.

During the time Moses led the Church in the desert, he experienced all kinds of attacks upon him:

- The people disparaged him (Exodus 32: 1) and spoke against him (Numbers 21: 4-5).

- His own brother and his sister-in-law criticised him (and his wife) and undermined his leadership (Numbers 12: 1-16).

- The people complained that they were better off dead and desired a different leader (Numbers 14: 1-4).

- They refused to heed his word (Numbers 14: 39-45, Deuteronomy 1: 41-46).

- Some of his fellow leaders 'became insolent and rose up against [him]' (Numbers 16: 1-2)[8].

The Holy Spirit, speaking later through the martyr Stephen, noted the rebellious attitude of the Church to Moses, despite the fact that he was a prophet of Christ:

This is the Moses who told the Israelites, "God will raise up for you a prophet like me from your own people" [Deuteronomy 18: 15]. He was in the assembly in the wilderness, with the angel who spoke to him on Mount Sinai, and with our ancestors; and he received living words to pass on to us. But our ancestors refused to obey him. Instead, they rejected him and, in their hearts, turned back to Egypt. (Acts 7: 37-39)

---

8   See also 2 Timothy 3: 8-9 which notes another incident when Moses is opposed (possibly referring to Numbers 16).

Coping with rebellion

It must have been difficult for Moses to experience this rejection of his leadership. He would have expected opposition from Pharaoh. It was of no surprise that an Egyptian king should reject the LORD and attack the leader of His Church but it must have been much more difficult for Moses to face opposition from his own people, even his own flesh and blood. It must have felt so much more personal. There must have been a sense of betrayal. *It's me they don't like. They hate me. They even prefer Pharaoh as leader to me.*

So how did Moses cope with the rebellion of the Israelites against him? First, he was a very humble man – 'more humble than anyone else on the face of the earth' (Numbers 12: 3). He did not think, when the Israelites grumbled, '*Well, it can't be anything to do with the way I am doing things. My leadership is perfect.*' He did not try to justify his way of doing things: to prove that he was right.

Moses' disappointment about the grumbling in the Church was driven by concern for the LORD's name, not his own. 'Why do you quarrel with me?' he said to those moaning (Exodus 17: 2). Yet he added, 'Why do you put *the LORD* to the test?' Moses must have been tempted towards self-pity, anger even, but the anger that he showed at the attacks on his leadership was a righteous anger for the glory of the LORD's name. His leadership was all about serving the LORD; he did nothing of himself; he said only the words of God; he did only what God commanded.

Moses was humble *because* he knew his flaws. Moses knew that he had nothing to commend himself to the Three Persons of God; that he gained his life from the sacrifice of *the* Passover Lamb – as had been demonstrated so graphically in the redemption of Israel from Egypt. He knew that he was saved from the wrath of God not because of *his* merits, but because of the blood of the Lamb. He knew also that to follow the Lamb meant to follow in His way of undeserved suffering.

And so Moses was not concerned to protect his reputation. As much as possible, he sought to leave his self out of his leadership.[9] He did not fight back against his critics. Neither did he seek to assert his personal authority; nor create his own clique of supporters to boost his power base. His leadership was about serving the LORD not advancing his own agenda.

Second, rooted in this humility, Moses did not seek to deal with the attacks against him in his own strength. Whenever he faced opposition from within the Church, he took the problem to God Most High through the Angel of the LORD who accompanied Israel in the desert. When the people grumbled about their lack of water, 'Moses cried out to the LORD, 'What am I to do with these people? They are almost ready to stone me' (Exodus 17: 4).

Moses knew that God Most High could only be approached because of the Passover Lamb; and yet because he related to the Father through the Lamb not his own merits, he knew he could approach the Father *with boldness.*

This is what the Triune God had taught Moses when the Angel had stood in the fire of God's wrath[10]. And He repeated

---

9   The LORD rebuked Moses on the couple of occasions when he did allow self to intrude into his leadership – when he used self-pity to reject his call to lead the Church (Ex 4: 1-14) and when his personal anger led him not to trust the LORD (Num 20: 1-13). At every other time, the LORD supported Moses' leadership.

10   Exodus 3: 1-6

the lesson at greater length when Moses ascended Mount Sinai. There, God Most High let Moses see ahead the saving works of Christ, and commanded him to copy them in the building of the tabernacle and to write about in the Law.[11] The prophet was shown that there was a way to enter the Most Holy Place and relate to God Most High: it was through the Great High Priest.

In the tabernacle, the High Priest could enter the Most Holy Place through the blood of the sacrifices. The sacrifices had to be made on a regular basis, demonstrating that they were not the means of salvation; but they prophesied Christ, the High Priest, who would enter 'the Most Holy Place once for all by his own blood, so obtaining eternal redemption'[12].

Moses looked ahead and saw the sacrificed yet risen Jesus ascending to heaven – enjoying fellowship with God Most High, re-uniting God and man, crushing His enemies under his feet.[13] Trusting in the ascended Christ, Moses could himself enter the Most Holy Place. He believed what he had seen on the mountain – that God would raise him up with Christ and seat him in the heavenly realms[14]. Knowing that he had a 'Great Priest over the house of God', Moses could 'draw near to God with a sincere heart and with the full assurance that faith brings'. [15]

And so Moses took all his concerns, complaints, requests and petitions to God Most High through the LORD Jesus Christ. He did not face his opposition alone, but in fellowship

---

11   Exodus 25: 40 and Hebrews 8: 5.

12   Hebrews 9: 13. Hebrews 7-10 provide a commentary on how the tabernacle was pointing to the work of Christ.

13   Moses shows his faith in the ascension of Christ in Numbers 10: 33-36 (see Psalm 68: 1, 18, Ephesians 4: 7-13).

14   Ephesians 2: 6

15   Hebrews 10: 19-21.

with God the Father, Son and Spirit. Even when Moses was at breaking point – and wanted to end his life – he still turned to the Angel of the LORD, pouring out his rawest emotions:

> He asked the LORD, 'Why have you brought this trouble on your servant? What have I done to displease you that you put the burden of all these people on me? Did I conceive all these people? Did I give them birth? Why do you tell me to carry them in my arms, as a nurse carries an infant, to the land you promised on oath to their ancestors? Where can I get meat for all these people? They keep wailing to me, "Give us meat to eat!" I cannot carry all these people by myself; the burden is too heavy for me. If this is how you are going to treat me, please go ahead and kill me right now – if I have found favour in your eyes – and do not let me face my own ruin'. (Numbers 11: 11-15)

Only someone who was truly humble before the true and living God – and utterly confident in their salvation in Christ – could dare to talk so boldly to Him.

Third, Moses coped with the attacks upon him because he loved the people who opposed him. He did not think that they were 'worse sinners' than he was. If he could be saved, they could be. They were not beyond God's love. Christ the High Priest was to sacrifice Himself for their sins as much as his. As God Most High loved him, despite his sin, because of Christ, so he loved them, even when they grumbled and spoke against him; even when they were near to stoning him.

Yes, Moses got angry with the Israelites; he felt despair when they rebelled against the LORD Jesus time and time again; and yet they were *his* people. His leadership was about serving them not using them to gain his own advantage. He got angry with them because he cared for them. Had he been complacent about their sin or wanted to avoid any conflict, he could have let the people carry on defying the LORD. But he cared too much about them to be quiet. He poured himself out for them. He pleaded on their behalf with the LORD, urging that they might be spared punishment; even being prepared – after the Israelites had built a golden calf as an idol – to forego his own salvation that they might be saved:

> Moses went back to the LORD and said, 'Oh, what a great sin these people have committed! They have made themselves gods of gold. But now, please forgive their sin – but if not, then blot me out of the book you have written (Exodus 32: 31-32)[16].

To Moses, the people were not just a problem to solve; an irritation to overcome; a threat to his way of doing things; an opposition to defeat. They were lost, needy, broken individuals: sheep who needed shepherding. Following the example of Christ, Moses was prepared to sacrifice himself for them:

> '...once again I fell prostrate before the LORD for forty days and forty nights; I ate no bread and drank no water, because of all the sin you had committed, doing what was evil in the LORD's sight and so arousing his anger. I feared the anger and wrath of the LORD, for he was angry enough with you to destroy you. But again the LORD listened to me. And the LORD was angry enough with Aaron to destroy him, but at that time I prayed for

---

16 The apostle Paul shows the same sacrificial attitude as Moses in Romans 9: 1-4.

Aaron too. Also I took that sinful thing of yours, the calf you had made, and burned it in the fire. Then I crushed it and ground it to powder as fine as dust and threw the dust into a stream that flowed down the mountain...

I lay prostrate before the LORD those forty days and forty nights because the LORD had said he would destroy you. I prayed to the Lord and said, 'Sovereign LORD, do not destroy your people, your own inheritance that you redeemed by your great power and brought out of Egypt with a mighty hand. Remember your servants Abraham, Isaac and Jacob. Overlook the stubbornness of this people, their wickedness and their sin. Otherwise, the country from which you brought us will say, "Because the LORD was not able to take them into the land he had promised them, and because he hated them, he brought them out to put them to death in the wilderness." But they are your people, your inheritance that you brought out by your great power and your outstretched arm.' (Deuteronomy 9: 18-29).

Holding out the Gospel

Moses faithfully showed the love of the Triune God to the Israelites even when they rejected his leadership. And so, back in Rephidim in Exodus 17, after Moses had taken the people's complaints about their lack of water to the LORD, he acted in obedience to what the LORD commanded:

The LORD answered Moses, 'Go out in front of the people. Take with you some of the elders of Israel and take in your hand the staff with which you struck the Nile, and go. I will stand there before you by the rock at Horeb. Strike the rock, and water will come out of it for the people to drink.' So Moses did this in the sight of the elders of Israel. (Exodus 17: 5-6).

The LORD did not allow Moses to deal with the people alone; He publicly backed Moses in front of the people; standing with the prophet as he struck the rock from which the water issued. The LORD graciously provided for the people, despite their rejection of Him. In His mercy, He did not chastise the people; they were given what they asked for; and yet beyond that they were being offered what they really needed – the life that there was in Him. They were given a sign which pointed them to *Him*. The staff of wood gave them life-giving water, as it had given them saving life when it had struck the Nile.[17] The LORD's concern was that the people would understand their need to drink from Him – the LORD Jesus Christ who was 'the spiritual rock that accompanied them' (1 Corinthians 10: 3-4). Their souls needed His spiritual water far more than the water which gushed out of the rock.

Moses faithfully struck the rock to teach the people that they needed to drink from the LORD Jesus. And throughout the time in the desert, Moses was a faithful servant of the gospel of Christ[18], seeking to focus the people on Him by:

- Teaching the Law and administering the sacrifices which pointed to Christ.[19]

- Giving them signs of the eternal life which Christ's death on the tree would give them.[20]

---

17 The Israelites had already witnessed the significance of wood at Marah when a piece had turned bitter water into life-giving water (Exodus 15: 22-25). The wooden staff of God was central too in the defeat of the Amalekites – when Moses held up the wood to make a sign of a cross, with a man on either side of him (17: 8-16).

18 Hebrews 3: 1-6

19 Exodus 20-40, Romans 10: 4

20 Numbers 21: 4-9; John 3: 13-16

- Prophesying about Christ.[21]

- Preaching about the eternal life that was theirs if they trusted in the LORD Jesus[22].

Through this teaching ministry and his personal example, Moses sought to fix the Church's eyes on the LORD Jesus and turn them away from their grumbling about their temporal concerns. He wanted the Church to stop moaning to stop persecuting its leaders, and to live out its calling as a 'kingdom of priests and a holy nation'[23] – to be a witness to the nations around them, drawing them to the LORD.

Moses poured his energy into discipling Israel but he recognised the need for evangelism as well as discipleship. He recognised that not all of the visible Church in the desert were followers of the LORD Jesus; 'not all who are descended from Israel are Israel'. Moses knew that it was only those who have faith in Christ who are children of Abraham[24] – and so he pointed the Israelites to Christ.

At other times when the people grumbled and rebelled against the LORD and him, Moses was called to warn and discipline the people. He made clear the judgement that would fall upon them if they turned away from the LORD; he rebuked and judged the idolatrous and rebellious.[25] Yet, as we have seen, Moses did so not because he thought his leadership was perfect and beyond criticism, but because he shared the LORD's passionate concern that the people would turn to Him. Moses wasn't bothered about his own

21   Deuteronomy 18: 15, 18-19, Acts 3: 22-23

22   Deuteronomy 30: 11-15, Romans 10: 6-9

23   Exodus 19: 6

24   Romans 9: 6, Galatians 3: 7, 26-29

25   See Numbers 16

popularity. He cared too deeply for his people to care what they thought of him. He wanted them to repent; to be liberated from their sinful ways; to escape their slavery and become the people God wanted them to be. He wanted them to trust deeply in the LORD who was to sacrifice Himself for them, such that they were prepared to put to death their own sins and live for Him.

Moses was prepared to exercise discipline in the Church in order to help it keep its focus on the LORD Jesus. Moses wanted to protect his flock from the wolves promoting their own agenda – and who grumbled against him. He sought to keep the Church from those who, the Holy Spirit says, are:

> ...ungodly people, who pervert the grace of our God into a licence for immorality and deny Jesus Christ our only Sovereign and Lord... These people are grumblers and faultfinders; they follow their own evil desires; they boast about themselves and flatter others for their own advantage. (Jude v 4, 16)

Don't Forget

After giving the people the water from the rock, Moses gave signs to the Church in order that they should trust in the LORD Jesus and humbly depend upon on Him:

> He called the place Massah [Testing] and Meribah [Quarrelling] because the Israelites quarrelled and because they tested the LORD saying, 'Is the LORD among us or not?' (Exodus 17: 7)

Moses did not want the people to forget their sin, and the Holy Spirit reminded the Church in subsequent generations of the lessons of Massah and Meribah in order that God's people should be faithful to the LORD Jesus:

> Do not put the Lord your God to the test as you did at
> Massah. (Deuteronomy 6: 16)[26]

> Today, if only you would hear his voice, 'Do not harden
> your hearts as you did at Meribah, as you did that day at
> Massah in the wilderness, where your ancestors tested
> me; they tried me, though they had seen what I did'.
> (Psalm 95:7-9)

The Holy Spirit does not want the Church of God to rebel
against the LORD Jesus and resist the Spirit[27]. He wants us
to fulfil our calling to be Christ's witnesses to the world; not
spend our time grumbling about Him and our leaders. We
need each day to listen to Christ's voice and obey Him:

> As the Holy Spirit says: **'Today, if you hear [Christ's]
> voice**, do not harden your hearts as you did in the
> rebellion, during the time of testing in the wilderness,
> where your ancestors tested and tried me, though for
> forty years they saw what I did'... [Psalm 95:7-10]. See
> to it, brothers and sisters, that none of you has a sinful,
> unbelieving heart that turns away from the living God.
> But encourage one another daily, as long as it is called
> 'Today', so that none of you may be hardened by sin's
> deceitfulness. We have come to share in Christ, if indeed
> we hold our original conviction firmly to the very end. As
> has just been said: **'Today, if you hear His voice**, do not
> harden your hearts as you did in the rebellion.' (Hebrews
> 3: 7-9, 12-15)

The story of Massah and Meribah teaches us that Church
leaders must expect criticism, slander, and rebellion. If they
are faithful to the gospel of Christ they are likely to face

---

26   See also Deuteronomy 9: 22, 33: 8.

27   Acts 7: 51-53

opposition from within the Church as well as from without. Yet the story is a reminder to us all not to test the LORD and grumble against our Church leaders. The Scriptures record the events at Massah and Meribah so that we might heed Christ's voice and avoid the sin of grumbling. 'These things occurred as examples to keep us from setting our hearts on evil things as they did' (1 Corinthians 10: 6).

CHAPTER FOUR

PERSECUTION UNDER ISRAEL'S KING

The previous chapter noted the warnings given by the Holy Spirit about church members persecuting their leaders. This chapter focuses on church leaders' persecution of their members.

There are examples in every age of church leaders who expect the kind of allegiance from their members which should only be given to the LORD Jesus. Often this seems to arise because the members want their church to stand up to their political rulers or the influence of other religions, or to compete with other churches. The members demand strong leaders so that their church will be successful and powerful or, at the very least, won't get trampled on.

But strong leaders may then be tempted to abuse their position. There are plenty of church leaders who regard themselves as beyond criticism; who expect all their members to conform to their will; to share their opinion on every issue; and who slander those who don't. Such leaders will use any means to silence anyone they perceive not to be 'on their side'.

The Holy Spirit teaches us about this kind of persecution in the first book of Samuel.

Massacre of the Priests

Then the king sent for the priest Ahimelek son of Ahitub and all the men of his family, who were the priests at Nob, and they all came to the king. Saul said, 'Listen now, son of Ahitub.' 'Yes, my lord,' he answered.

Saul said to him, 'Why have you conspired against me, you and the son of Jesse, giving him bread and a sword and enquiring of God for him, so that he has rebelled against me and lies in wait for me, as he does today?'

Ahimelech answered the king, 'Who of all your servants is as loyal as David, the king's son-in-law, captain of your bodyguard and highly respected in your household? Was that day the first time I enquired of God for him? Of course not! Let not the king accuse your servant or any of his father's family, for your servant knows nothing at all about this whole affair.'

But the king said, 'You shall surely die, Ahimelech, you and your whole family.' Then the king ordered the guards at his side: 'Turn and kill the priests of the LORD, because they too have sided with David. They knew he was fleeing, yet they did not tell me.' But the king's officials were unwilling to raise a hand to strike the priests of the LORD.

The king then ordered Doeg, 'You turn and strike down the priests.' So Doeg the Edomite turned and struck them down. That day he killed eighty-five men who wore the linen ephod. He also put to the sword Nob, the town of the priests, with its men and women, its children and infants, and its cattle, donkeys and sheep' (1 Samuel 22: 11-19).

Once again the Church was under attack. The priests of Israel were brutally attacked and murdered by the king, along with everyone living in the town they inhabited. Did this incident take place back in Egypt, under a pagan king? Were the Israelites suffering under the hand of a ruler who did not know the Triune God? No. The king ordering the death of the priests in the above story was not an Egyptian but an Israelite! How was it that an Israelite king was persecuting his own people?[1] Indeed, how was it that Israel had a king at all?

Desiring a king

Moses had been appointed as leader of Israel by the Three Persons of God for a specific purpose for a specific time. God Most High had sent His Angel to rescue the nation out of Egypt. And the Angel of the LORD commissioned Moses to help Him in the task. Another leader, Joshua, was appointed for the purpose of taking Israel into Canaan, the Promised Land. Job done, Joshua sent the people to live in their inheritance in the land and he retired to his own allotment.[2] He did not hand on his leadership of the nation. There was no need for such a leader. There were all kinds of local leaders in the Church serving the people: elders; community leaders; judges; tribal heads[3]. They had a role in maintaining order within Israel and settling disputes between its members – for sinful humans invariably got into disputes[4]. But the LORD Jesus was the King of Israel.

---

1   The events of 1 Samuel 22 fulfil the prophecy given to Eli by the Holy Spirit in 1 Samuel 2: 27-36 about the destruction of his priestly house. But this does not absolve Saul of his responsibility for the massacre.

2   Joshua 19: 49-51, 24: 28

3   Numbers 1: 16, Deuteronomy 16: 18-20, Joshua 8: 13,

4   Exodus 18.

The people were called to worship Him, living out the commands given by Him through Moses.

Once Israel entered the Promised Land, it was supposed to be filled with the praise of the true and living God – and to be a picture of the new creation. For long periods this was the case and the people and land enjoyed peace and rest.[5] But at other times the Israelites were unfaithful. They worshipped other gods. So the LORD handed Israel over to foreign nations so they might see the error of their ways and turn to Him.

When the Israelites cried to God Most High in anguish, He sent His Angel and Spirit to save the Church, working through judges whom He raised up to turn the nation away from their idols and overthrow their foreign oppressors. Once their task was complete, the judges retired and the Church rested again in the land, ruled by the LORD.[6]

Yet the Israelites started to yearn for a ruler – a human ruler, one different from the LORD Jesus. They did not trust in Him to provide them with material comfort and security, so they looked for another.

Gideon was the first to be approached. He was one of the judges appointed by the LORD. His initial commission was to reform Israel – to remove its idols and false worship. Then he saved Israel from the Midianites, in a fantastic sign of the salvation that the LORD Jesus Christ would bring when He was born as a human being[7]. Being a freedom fighter made Gideon much more popular than being a Church reformer, and the Israelites said to him:

---

5   Judges 3: 11, 5: 31

6   See Judges 2: 10-19, a theme played out in the rest of the book.

7   See Isaiah's commentary on Judges 6-8 in Isaiah 9:1-7 and 10: 24-27.

'Rule over us—you, your son and your grandson—because you have saved us from the hand of Midian." But Gideon told them, 'I will not rule over you, nor will my son rule over you. The LORD will rule over you.' (Judges 8: 22-24)

Gideon made clear that the LORD Jesus was Israel's King. There could be no substitute; no pretender. There was no need or no room for Israel to have another Ruler. And yet, sometime later[8], after Samuel had become judge and prophet of Israel, events took a terrible turn:

When Samuel grew old, he appointed his sons as Israel's leaders. The name of his firstborn was Joel and the name of his second was Abijah, and they served at Beersheba. But his sons did not follow his ways. They turned aside after dishonest gain and accepted bribes and perverted justice.

So all the elders of Israel gathered together and came to Samuel at Ramah. They said to him, "You are old, and your sons do not follow your ways; now appoint a king to lead us, such as all the other nations have."

But when they said, "Give us a king to lead us," this displeased Samuel; so he prayed to the LORD. And the LORD told him: "Listen to all that the people are saying to you; it is not you they have rejected, but they have rejected me as their king. As they have done from the day I brought them up out of Egypt until this day, forsaking me and serving other gods, so they are doing to you" (1 Samuel 8: 1-8).

8   Israel did, in fact, have a brief (and disastrous) experiment with a king after Gideon had died (Judges 9).

On the surface, the people's request seemed commendable. They sought a leader like Samuel who was honest. They desired a land free of bribery and corruption. And they wanted a ruler to defend them. They had seen a neighbouring king moving against them[9], and wanted a protector: 'Then we shall be like all the other nations, with a king to lead us and to go out before us and fight our battles' (1 Samuel 8: 20).

Were these not good reasons to want a king? Surely the LORD Himself wanted them to be safe? To conquer His enemies? But the critical problem was that the desire of the people was to have good things without the LORD Jesus. Their desire was to have a king to rule over them 'even though the Lord their God was their king' (1 Samuel 12: 12).

Rejecting their King

In desiring a king, the people were not rejecting Samuel but the LORD. Their request for a human king was a symptom of their idolatry. The people wanted someone else other than the LORD Jesus on the throne.

They wanted to be like the pagan nations around them who seemed so powerful – even though they were ruled by kings who did not love and trust the Triune God.[10] Although the LORD Jesus had led the Israelites out of slavery in Egypt; had given them a land of milk and honey; had given them peace and security and justice; had handed them over

---

9   1 Samuel 12: 12.

10   Jeremiah 10: 1-10: 'Do not learn the ways of the nations... No one is like you, LORD... Among all the wise leaders of the nations and in all their kingdoms, there is no one like you. They are all senseless and foolish; they are taught by worthless wooden idols. But the LORD is the true God; he is the living God, the eternal King.

to their enemies when they rejected Him; had rescued them when they turned to Him in repentance: although they knew all those things, they did not trust Him to protect them.

Woe to those…
   who rely on horses,
who trust in the multitude of their chariots
   and in the great strength of their horsemen,
but do not look to the Holy One of Israel,
   or seek help from the LORD.
(Isaiah 31: 1)

Moses had given up the prestige and pleasures of Egypt to live for Christ; to suffer for Him and be one with His people[11]. Moses had turned his back on political power in order to serve the true King of the universe. Samuel followed Moses' example. Yet now the Israelites wanted a political ruler to give them influence in the world; to make their name mighty. They believed that the sword of their human king would make the nation great.

God the Father, through His Son and Spirit, had called the Israelites out of the nations on earth to be 'a kingdom of priests and a holy nation' (Exodus 19: 6). They were to be His ambassadors in the world, seeking to draw the nations to Him. The LORD told them that they 'must not live according to the customs of the nations: "You are to be holy to me because I, the LORD, am holy, and I have set you apart from the nations to be my own"'[12]. The LORD had set Israel apart be a witness to Him to the other nations, by following His decrees and laws:

---

11   Hebrews 11: 24-28

12   Leviticus 20: 23-26

Observe them carefully, for this will show your wisdom and understanding to the nations, who will hear about all these decrees and say, 'Surely this great nation is a wise and understanding people.' What other nation is so great as to have their gods near them the way the Lord our God is near us whenever we pray to him? And what other nation is so great as to have such righteous decrees and laws as this body of laws I am setting before you today? (Deuteronomy 4: 6-8)

If Israel wanted to be great, it did not need to follow a king into war against its neighbours; it needed to focus on showing 'wisdom and understanding'. Rather than being caught up in political intrigue and power, they were to love the true and living God with all their heart and soul, and to love their neighbours as themselves. In that way Israel would be a beacon of light to the nations around them such that they would want to join it and to love and serve the LORD Jesus. The world would change as the Church grew in number and filled the earth. If the Israelites wanted to see real transformation in the world around them, they needed to be a faithful witness to the LORD, not follow its agenda.

Israel's king

Although saddened at this rejection of His rule, the LORD granted the people's request. He told Samuel: 'Listen to them; but warn them solemnly and let them know what the king who will reign over them will claim as his rights' (1 Samuel 8: 9).

You can have what you desire, the LORD Jesus was saying. You can have your king. But be warned. Be very clear what the consequences will be if you put your trust in a sinful human being as king. You are creating a kind of idol.

You are worshipping human power and that power is not benign. It will be used against you. You are investing power into one flawed individual, and you will become his slaves. Human beings are self-centred and dishonest and greedy, and the more power you give them, the more likely they will exercise that power in a self-centred, dishonest and greedy way.

Through Samuel, the LORD prophesied exactly what to expect from their king:

> He will take your sons and make them serve with his chariots and horses, and they will run in front of his chariots. Some he will assign to be commanders of thousands and commanders of fifties, and others to plough his ground and reap his harvest, and still others to make weapons of war and equipment for his chariots. He will take your daughters to be perfumers and cooks and bakers. He will take the best of your fields and vineyards and olive groves and give them to his attendants. He will take a tenth of your grain and of your vintage and give it to his officials and attendants. Your male and female servants and the best of your cattle and donkeys he will take for his own use. He will take a tenth of your flocks, and you yourselves will become his slaves. (1 Samuel 8: 11-17)

The king the people wanted would not show the sacrificial love of the true King, the LORD Jesus. The king would serve himself not the people. The people should not put their 'trust in princes, in human beings, who cannot save'; they should not forget that 'It is better to take refuge in the LORD than to trust in humans. It is better to take refuge in the LORD than to trust in princes'.[13]

---

13   Psalm 146:3 and 118: 8-9

The day will come, Samuel said, when:
You will cry out for relief from the king you have chosen,
but the Lord will not answer you in that day.

But the people refused to listen to Samuel. 'No!' they
said. 'We want a king over us. Then we shall be like all
the other nations, with a king to lead us and to go out
before us and fight our battles.' When Samuel heard all
that the people said, he repeated it before the Lord. The
Lord answered, 'Listen to them and give them a king'
(1 Samuel 8: 18-22).

The people were obstinate in their rejection of the LORD
Jesus. And He granted them their sinful desire to have a
king. Later, the LORD looked back on this moment in
Israel's history and said: 'In my anger, I gave you a king...'
(Hosea 13:11).

There is nothing more terrifying than when the LORD
allows people to go their own way.

King Saul

The introduction of a king created confusion over Israel's
identity. It had been called to be the people of the Triune
God; its life was supposed to be focused on the sacrifices
and priests which pointed them to the Messiah. Yet now
Israel was also a kingdom ruled by a king with his own
interests and agenda, surrounded by his advisors and army.

The LORD made clear that it was 'good' if the people
and the king who reigned over them were faithful to Him and
if they obeyed the laws pointing to the Messiah[14]. The king
of Israel could act as a shadow of the true Divine King of
Israel. To do so, the king must respect the limited remit he

---

14   1 Samuel 12: 13-14 cf Deuteronomy 17: 14-20.

held within Israel. He might have some useful role in curbing evil. But only the Messiah could *vanquish* evil. It was not for the king to interfere with the laws given to Israel which taught them about the Messiah; his job was, along with everyone else, to obey them. The risk, as Samuel had warned, was that the king would be concerned with protecting his own power and wealth rather than honouring the LORD.

A king would be deemed to be successful not in relation to the number of battles he won but on the basis of his faithfulness to the LORD Jesus. Jesus is the 'stone that causes people to stumble'[15]. All the Israelite kings would be judged according to their attitude to Christ, evidenced in whether they observed the laws given by the LORD about the altar, sacrifices, and priests.[16] Did they have faith in the Passover Lamb, who would be slaughtered on the altar? Did they believe that there was nothing they could do in the face of the Triune God's hatred of wickedness but to place their sins on the Lamb and trust that **He** would deal with them? Were they prepared to deposit their self on the altar and trust in the sacrificed Lamb? Did they have faith that the Great High Priest could make them one with God Most High? Or did they trust in their own righteousness? Did they believe they could please God Most High through their own works rather than trusting in the High Priest offering *Himself*? [17]

---

15   See Isaiah 8:14, Isaiah 28:16, Psalm 118:22, 1 Peter 2:1-8.

16   In the books of Kings and Chronicles, the Holy Spirit mainly characterises the kings of Israel and Judah according to their attitude to the sacrifices – and thus the Sacrificial Lamb of God. The kings of the world are also judged according to their attitude to Christ i.e. whether they desire to 'kiss the Son' (Psalm 2: 10-12).

17   Leviticus 1: 1-9, Leviticus 16: 6-10, 15-22

Saul, Israel's first king, who ruled in Israel for around 40 years, appeared to follow this latter way: seeking to win the favour of God through his own deeds. Superficially, he tried to follow the LORD Jesus and yet his faith was deeply compromised. He could not resist the temptation to serve his own interests. He had a 'form of godliness whilst denying its power'.[18] His heart was more concerned with advancing his own agenda than serving the true King.[19]

Moses and Joshua worshipped the LORD Jesus when He helped them defeat the enemies of the Church; and they urged their fellow Israelites to love and trust Him[20]. When the LORD helped Saul to defeat Israel's enemies, the Amalekites, the king 'set up a monument **in his own honour**' (1 Samuel 15: 12). Saul wanted people to praise him. He desired that they give glory to him.

In an earlier battle – before the one with the Amalekites – Saul had shown his disrespect for the High Priest by assuming himself the role of priest, in defiance of the laws of Moses, and offering up burnt offerings to God.[21] It was not his right, whether king or not, to usurp the role of the ones who foreshadowed *the* High Priest.

And after the conquest of the Amalekites, Saul disobeyed the LORD's command to destroy all their power and evil, and sought to cover his rebellion against God Most High by

---

18   2 Timothy 3: 5

19   This is not to say that Saul did not have a saving faith in the LORD Jesus. In David's lament for Saul on his death he refers to his predecessor as the 'glory' of Israel and praises his graciousness and courage (2 Samuel 1: 17-27). Through the Holy Spirit, David forgets Saul's sins and failures but sees him as he is in Christ. What a relief for followers of Christ that the Triune God overlooks the sins of our time on earth.

20   See Exodus 15 and Joshua 24

21   1 Samuel 13: 1-14.

using religious offerings to earn His favour[22]. Yet, as the prophet told him:

> Does the LORD delight in burnt offerings and sacrifices as much as in obeying the LORD? To obey is better than sacrifice, and to heed is better than the fat of rams. For rebellion is like the sin of divination, and arrogance like the evil of idolatry. (1 Samuel 15: 22-23)

Only the sacrifice of Jesus could earn the favour of God Most High. It pleased the Father if an animal sacrifice was brought to Him *with* faith in Christ. The Israelites were being obedient if they made their offerings with such faith. It was sheer arrogance to think that they could please God Most High by making a burnt offering *without* faith in the Lamb of God.

In contrast to Moses, Saul was obsessed by self. He was jealous of others being successful; concerned about his own standing; worried about what people thought of him. His political decisions were often fuelled by insecurity[23]. Personal vulnerability lurked behind his dictatorial approach. He flicked between self-importance and self-pity[24]. Everything was self.

A persecuting king

What did all this mean for Saul's kingship? It meant he viewed every person and event through a single perspective: *Does this boost my power? Yes or No?*

Saul showed little interest in whether the members of Israel were serving the LORD Jesus or loving their neighbour. His interest was 'Are you for me or not?' And if they were

---

22   1 Samuel 15: 1-21.

23   1 Samuel 15: 24

24   1 Samuel 22: 6-8

not for him, they were his enemies, whether or not they were part of the people of God, united in the blood of the Lamb.

Saul was thus driven to persecute fellow members of Israel, and it was David whom was the chief object of his hatred. Saul had brought David into his court because he believed he would be a useful asset against Israel's enemies. Yet David's very success in battle made Saul mad with jealousy:

> Whatever mission Saul sent him on, David was so successful that Saul gave him a high rank in the army. This pleased all the troops, and Saul's officers as well. When the men were returning home after David had killed the Philistine, the women came out from all the towns of Israel to meet King Saul with singing and dancing, with joyful songs and with tambourines and lyres. As they danced, they sang: 'Saul has slain his thousands, and David his tens of thousands.'

> Saul was very angry; this refrain displeased him greatly. 'They have credited David with tens of thousands,' he thought, 'but me with only thousands. What more can he get but the kingdom?' And from that time on Saul kept a close eye on David.

> ...In everything [David] did he had great success, because the LORD was with him. When Saul saw how successful he was, he was afraid of him. But all Israel and Judah loved David, because he led them in their campaigns. (1 Samuel 18: 5-9, 14-16).

Saul's jealousy became even deeper when David was anointed king instead of him[25]. Rather than humbly

---

25 Saul had been told at an earlier stage that the kingship was being given to someone else – 1 Samuel 13:4. See also 1 Samuel 16.

acknowledge the LORD's choice, Saul fought against it.[26] He clung to power and tried to kill David.[27] Anyone who Saul thought was a threat to his political authority was a legitimate subject of attack. Even his own son, Jonathan, was subject to his suspicion. Saul said to him:

> You son of a perverse and rebellious woman! Don't I know that you have sided with the son of Jesse to your own shame and to the shame of the mother who bore you? As long as the son of Jesse lives on this earth, neither you nor your kingdom will be established. Now send someone to bring him to me, for he must die! (1 Samuel 20: 30-31).

Jonathan showed the sacrificial love of the LORD Jesus to David, loving the future king as himself as a fellow believer in the LORD.[28] They were united by the blood of the Lamb of God. Yet for Saul, anyone who was for David was against him. And David himself had to escape the court of Saul and run like an animal across Israel to escape capture by the king and his army.

The Priests of Nob

All this is the background to the incident recorded at the start of this chapter – the extraordinary story described in 1 Samuel 22 in which the king of Israel ordered the murder of the priests of Nob. David, on the run from Saul, had previously gone to Nob in search of food and a weapon. Clearly worried about whom he could trust (and showing that he was a sinner like everyone else), David lied to Ahimelech, the priest, pretending he was on mission

---

26   In contrast, David respected Saul as the anointed one of the LORD (see 1 Samuel 24 and 26).

27   1 Samuel 18: 10-11; 19: 1-10 etc.

28   1 Samuel 20: 42.

authorised by Saul. After David had been given what he needed by Ahimelech, he moved on. But he had been spotted by one of Saul's henchmen, Doeg the Edomite, who told Saul. And so:

> ...the king sent for the priest Ahimelech son of Ahitub and all the men of his family, who were the priests at Nob, and they all came to the king. Saul said, "Listen now, son of Ahitub." "Yes, my lord," he answered. Saul said to him, "Why have you conspired against me, you and the son of Jesse, giving him bread and a sword and inquiring of God for him, so that he has rebelled against me and lies in wait for me, as he does today?' (1 Samuel 22: 11-13).

Again, Saul's only concern was whether Ahimelech was loyal to him or not. The priest pleaded his case:

> Ahimelech answered the king, 'Who of all your servants is as loyal as David, the king's son-in-law, captain of your bodyguard and highly respected in your household? Was that day the first time I inquired of God for him? Of course not! Let not the king accuse your servant or any of his father's family, for your servant knows nothing at all about this whole affair'. (14-15)

But Saul demanded total allegiance:

> 'You will surely die, Ahimelech, you and your whole family.' Then the king ordered the guards at his side: 'Turn and kill the priests of the LORD, because they too have sided with David. They knew he was fleeing, yet they did not tell me'. (16-17).

The king's officials were, however, 'unwilling to raise a hand to strike the priests of the Lord'. They had too much respect for these representatives of *the* High Priest. But Saul was not defeated:

> The king then ordered Doeg, 'You turn and strike down the priests.' So Doeg the Edomite turned and struck them down. That day he killed eighty-five men who wore the linen ephod. He also put to the sword Nob, the town of the priests, with its men and women, its children and infants, and its cattle, donkeys and sheep (18-19).

Some followers of the LORD Jesus Christ know that their actions are likely to lead to their being martyred. The fate of other Christian believers is to suffer for being in the wrong place at the wrong time. The priests of Nob had not woken up that morning knowing their lives were in danger; that martyrdom was their fate. But suddenly, as might happen to any follower of the LORD, the priests were caught up in the state's attempt to persecute a fellow believer. They were called to denounce him in order to demonstrate their loyalty to the king. To do anything else could put their own lives at risk.

What a choice. But their spokesman, Ahimelech, trusted in the LORD Jesus and simply told the truth when questioned by Saul. He did not fear the king; he feared the true King of Israel.

But that was exactly the problem for Saul. He demanded complete fidelity; he didn't allow room for loyalty to anyone else – human or divine. Saul had made himself god. The priests of Nob *had* to die: they were representatives of the Triune God – the Being who had rejected him for David.

> [Saul] seems well pleased with this opportunity of being revenged on the priests of the Lord, since God himself was out of his reach. What wickedness will not the evil spirit hurry men to, when he gets the dominion![29]

29 Henry, op cit, 422.

Saul murdered the priests in order to preserve his power; to maintain his god-like status. Such was his blindness that he appeared to think that shedding the priests' blood could save him; that their blood would preserve his life. Yet the very purpose of the priests was to remind Israel that it was the blood of the Lamb of God which was required for salvation. In *His* blood was life.[30] In seeking his own salvation, Saul had just destroyed the witness to the true means of salvation.

The blood of the priests fell to the ground – part of 'all the righteous blood that has been shed on earth'[31]. Apart from Ahimelech, their names are unknown to us, but not to the true and living God. He never forgets them; their blood continues to cry out to Him.

Saul gave half-hearted attempts to repent for his sins[32]; but he could not rid himself of his desire to be his own king; his own god. His thirst for political power always compromised his love for the LORD Jesus and His people.

Godly leaders

Saul had started his reign with the LORD Jesus Christ at the centre of the nation, and with the people celebrating his anointing as king[33]. Over time, as he became obsessed by his own power, he led people further and further away from LORD, and the kingdom was dominated by violence and conflict.

The Israelites had wanted a king like the other nations. And in doing so, they became a people like the other nations

---

30   Leviticus 17: 11

31   Matthew 23: 25

32   1 Samuel 26: 21

33   1 Samuel 11: 12-15

– who turned their back on the LORD Jesus and were obsessed by power and violence.

1 Samuel provides a warning to the Church in every age: to avoid the temptation to be like the world and have faith in sinful human power. And it provides a warning, through the story of Saul, of the temptation upon church leaders to use power to serve their own interests.

Saul reigned over God's people for 40 years; yet he is only remembered in the Scriptures for his persecution of his own people.[34]

The leaders of the Church are not to wield power over their congregations. Their task is to help and support their fellow Church members to serve the Triune God and each other. Their calling is to follow the example of the LORD Jesus Christ, the Divine King, not to be like the kings of the nations:

> Then James and John, the sons of Zebedee, came to [the LORD Jesus]. 'Teacher,' they said, 'we want you to do for us whatever we ask.' 'What do you want me to do for you?' he asked. They replied, 'Let one of us sit at your right and the other at your left in your glory.' 'You don't know what you are asking,' Jesus said. 'Can you drink the cup I drink or be baptised with the baptism I am baptised with?' 'We can,' they answered. Jesus said to them, 'You will drink the cup I drink and be baptised with the baptism I am baptised with, but to sit at my right or left is not for me to grant. These places belong to those for whom they have been prepared.'
>
> When the ten heard about this, they became indignant with James and John. Jesus called them together and

---

34   See Psalm 18:1, 52:1, 54:1, 57:1, 59:1

said, 'You know that those who are regarded as rulers of the Gentiles lord it over them, and their high officials exercise authority over them. Not so with you. Instead, whoever wants to become great among you must be your servant, and whoever wants to be first must be slave of all. For even the Son of Man did not come to be served, but to serve, and to give his life as a ransom for many.' (Mark 10: 35-45)[35]

---

35   See 1 Peter 5: 1-4.

CHAPTER FIVE

PSALMS OF THE PERSECUTED

Is it possible to find hope and encouragement when you are attacked for being a follower of Christ? Your door has been beaten down, you have been assaulted, your spouse and children taken away. Can you find any comfort? In the midst of the pain and fear what comes into your mind? What words can you find to pray?

Those who have spent many years reading and singing the Psalms testify that at times of suffering those songs flood into their souls. The Psalms help Christians to endure persecution because so many of them are about how Christ depended on His Father in the light of *His* suffering. The longest Psalm in the Psalms – Psalm 119 – prophesies Jesus' reliance on His Father; His attentiveness to His Father's commands, and His desire to do His will. Christ's obsession with His Father's words helped Him to bear the persecution He faced:

Rulers persecute me without cause,
    but my heart trembles at your word.
I rejoice in your promise
    like one who finds great spoil.
I hate and detest falsehood
    but I love your law.
Seven times a day I praise you
    for your righteous laws.
Great peace have those who love your law,
    and nothing can make them stumble.

> I wait for your salvation, Lord,
>   and I follow your commands.
> I obey your statutes,
>   for I love them greatly.
> I obey your precepts and your statutes,
>   for all my ways are known to you.
> (Psalm 119: 161-8)[1]
>
> This chapter reflects on how the Church can endure its persecution in the light of the glory of Jesus' suffering.

David: the Prophet of Christ

As noted in the previous chapter, David spent many years on the run from king Saul. David suffered persecution because his King was the LORD Jesus Christ; and Saul did not want any rivals to his own kingship.

What sustained David during these times of persecution? What kept him going when Saul and his army hunted him down like an animal?

He sang songs.

He didn't hum a few ditties to try and keep his spirits up. He sang truths about the Triune God. When David was being pursued by king Saul's henchman (Doeg) – the story covered in the last chapter – he sang the following song, expressing his hope in his LORD[2]:

---

1   For a few examples of the way this passage is fulfilled in Christ's life after He took human flesh see Mark 1: 35, Matthew 27: 27-31 and Luke 5: 15-16, 6: 12.

2   For the background to the Psalm see 1 Samuel 21-22. Saul is specifically mentioned in the introduction to four of David's other Psalms: Psalms 18, 54, 57 and 59. Many of the Psalms were written by David whilst on the run from his enemies: 7, 11-13,16-17,22, 25,31, 34-35, 53, 56, 58, 63-64, 142-143.

Why do you boast of evil, you mighty hero?
    Why do you boast all day long,
    you who are a disgrace in the eyes of God?
You who practise deceit,
    your tongue plots destruction;
    it is like a sharpened razor.
You love evil rather than good,
    falsehood rather than speaking the truth.
You love every harmful word,
    you deceitful tongue!
Surely God will bring you down to everlasting ruin:
    he will snatch you up and pluck you from your tent;
    he will uproot you from the land of the living.
The righteous will see and fear;
    they will laugh at you, saying,
'Here now is the man
    who did not make God his stronghold
but trusted in his great wealth
    and grew strong by destroying others!'
But I am like an olive tree
    flourishing in the house of God;
I trust in God's unfailing love
    for ever and ever.
For what you have done I will always praise you
    in the presence of your faithful people.
And I will hope in your name,
    for your name is good
(Psalm 52)

David was Israel's 'singer of songs'. As he looked back on his life, he said: 'The Spirit of the LORD spoke through me; His word was on my tongue' (2 Sam 23: 1-2).

And, as Jonathan Edwards says, the way that the Spirit influenced David's singing was by:

> Inspiring him to show forth Christ, and the glorious things of His redemption, in divine songs, sweetly expressing the breathings of a pious soul, full of admiration of the glorious things of the Redeemer, inflamed with divine love and elevated praise; and therefore he is called the sweet psalmist of Israel...

> The main subjects of these songs were the glorious things of the gospel... Joyfully did this holy man sing of those great things of Christ's redemption, that had been the hope and expectation of God's church and people from the beginning; and joyfully did others follow him in it, as Asaph, Heman, Ethan, and others; for the book of Psalms was not all penned by David, though the greater part of it was.

> ... [In the Psalms] Christ is spoken of by his ancestor David abundantly, in multitudes of songs, speaking of his incarnation, life, death, resurrection, ascension into heaven, his satisfaction, intercession; his prophetical, kingly, and priestly office; his glorious benefits in this life and that which is to come; his union with the church, and the blessedness of the church in him; the calling of the Gentiles, the future glory of the church near the end of the world, and Christ's coming to the final judgment. All these things, and many more, concerning Christ and his redemption, are abundantly spoken of in the book of Psalms.[3]

The Psalms are the Psalms of Christ, spoken prophetically by David and the other human authors:

---

3   Jonathan Edwards, op cit

David was a prophet and knew that God had promised him on oath that he would place one of his descendants on his throne. Seeing what was to come, he spoke of the resurrection of the Messiah, that he was not abandoned to the realm of the dead, nor did his body see decay'. (Acts 2: 30-31)[4]

David saw 'what was to come' i.e. the Spirit enabled him to see ahead to when the LORD Jesus took human flesh. David could see the future saving work of Christ as though it was happening right before him and was able to write down for the Church what the incarnate LORD Jesus would experience and say. David was an eye witness of Christ's work. Moses set out what he had been shown of Christ in the Tabernacle and the Law. David wrote his prophetic visions of Christ in the Psalms.

Christ the Persecuted

Through the Holy Spirit, David and the other prophets 'predicted the sufferings of the Messiah and the glories that would follow' (1 Peter 1: 11[5]). Christ was to achieve glorious things: He would conquer sin and death; and secure eternal life in a glorious new creation. But the price of those things was His suffering. This King would not exert power over people or force His will upon them. Rather He would come to serve them; to lay down His life for them. The Son of God *must* suffer; then there would be glory.

The Psalms lay bare the persecution which the incarnate Jesus would experience at the hands of those opposed to

---

4   In 2 Samuel 7: 11-16, David is told that he was to be an ancestor of Christ, who would sit on his throne.

5   See Acts 3: 18

the true and living God. For example, the Scriptures foretold that lies would be told about Him:

> People who are wicked and deceitful
>> have opened their mouths against me;
>> they have spoken against me with lying tongues.
> With words of hatred they surround me;
>> they attack me without cause.[6]

Christ would be betrayed by one of His one close friends:

> Even my close friend,
>> someone I trusted,
> one who shared my bread,
>> has turned against me.[7]

His enemies would surround Him and attack Him; He would be mocked and ridiculed by crowds of people[8]. He would be 'hated without reason'[9]. And finally, he would be subject to an awful public death – a crucifixion. This is prophesied at greatest length in Psalm 22:

> I am a worm and not a man,
>> scorned by everyone, despised by the people.
> All who see me mock me;
>> they hurl insults, shaking their heads.
> 'He trusts in the LORD,' they say,
>> 'let the LORD rescue him.
> Let him deliver him,
>> since he delights in him.'
> Many bulls surround me;
>> strong bulls of Bashan encircle me.

---

6   Psalm 109: 2-3 cf Psalm 35: 11-12, Mathew 26: 59-80

7   Psalm 41:9 and 55: 12 cf Matthew 26: 20-25.

8   Psalm 109: 25 cf Matthew 27: 39-43

9   Psalm 35: 19 and 69: 4, 19-21, cf John 15: 25. Matthew 27: 34, John 19: 28-29.

Roaring lions that tear their prey
>   open their mouths wide against me.
I am poured out like water,
>   and all my bones are out of joint.
My heart has turned to wax;
>   it has melted within me.
My mouth is dried up like a potsherd,
>   and my tongue sticks to the roof of my mouth;
>   you lay me in the dust of death.
Dogs surround me,
>   a pack of villains encircles me;
>   they pierce my hands and my feet.
All my bones are on display;
>   people stare and gloat over me.
They divide my clothes among them
>   and cast lots for my garment'
(Psalm 22: 6-18)[10]

Enduring Persecution

How would Christ be able to endure such unjust suffering?

The Psalms prophesied that the LORD Jesus would face His persecution with complete trust in His Father, a trust which was built through His immersion in the Scriptures and His regular times of prayer to His Father:

I rise before dawn and cry for help;
>   I have put my hope in your word.
My eyes stay open through the watches of the night,
>   that I may meditate on your promises.
Seven times a day I praise you
>   for your righteous laws.
(Psalm 119: 147, 148, 164)[11]

---

10   See Mark 15: 16-36.

11   See footnote 1

Christ was willing to fulfil all that the Psalms (and other Scriptures) had said about Him, in obedience to His Father:

'Sacrifice and offering you did not desire –
   but my ears you have opened; –
   burnt offerings and sin offerings you did not require.
Then I said, 'Here I am, I have come –
   it is written about me in the scroll.
I desire to do your will, my God;
   your law is within my heart'
(Psalm 40: 6-8).

Christ knew that His loving Father would see Him through His suffering, even as He faced the agony of His separation from Him. Out of the Triune God's love for humanity, Christ took the penalty of humanity's sin and was alienated from His eternal fellowship with His Father. The LORD Jesus experienced the reality of hell: estrangement from His Father:

My God, my God, why have you forsaken me?
   Why are you so far from saving me,
   so far from my cries of anguish?
My God, I cry out by day, but you do not answer,
   by night, but I find no rest
(Psalm 22: 1-5).[12]

Yet Christ still trusted His Father. In Psalm 22, immediately after crying out to the Father that He has forsaken Him, Christ would say:

---

12   See Matthew 27:45-46 and Hebrews 5: 7: 'During the days of Jesus' life on earth, he offered up prayers and petitions with loud cries and tears to the one who could save him from death, and he was heard because of his reverent submission.'

> **Yet** you are enthroned as the Holy One;
>> you are the one Israel praises.
> In you our ancestors put their trust;
>> they trusted and you delivered them
> To you they cried out and were saved;
>> in you they trusted and were not put to shame.
> (Psalm 22: 3-5).

The LORD Jesus knew that His Father was enthroned in heaven 'as the Holy One'. He trusted in His Father's goodness and power and salvation.

The prophecy of Christ's suffering in Psalm 22 testifies to His faith in His Father. Christ would endure mocking by His enemies (v7). **Yet** He knew that His eternal Father would look after Him as He had done since His birth as a human being:

> ...you brought me out of the womb;
>> you made me trust in you, even at my mother's
> breast.
> From birth I was cast on you;
>> from my mother's womb you have been my God.

And so Jesus could ask His Father with confidence:

> Do not be far from me,
>> for trouble is near
>> and there is no one to help.
> (Psalm 22: 9-11)

Wild dogs would tear Christ apart (v13). **But** He knew His Father remained close to Him:

> ...you, Lord, do not be far from me.
>> You are my strength; come quickly to help me.
> Deliver me from the sword,

my precious life from the power of the dogs.
Rescue me from the mouth of the lions;
    save me from the horns of the wild oxen.
(Psalm 22: 19-21)

The LORD trembled at the thought of His death and cried out to His Father to be rescued. Yet death was His destiny – that was His Father's answer[13].

Trusting in the power and goodness of His Father, Christ knew He could give His life to Him as it ebbed away:

'Into your hands I commit my spirit;
 deliver me, LORD, my faithful God'
(Psalm 31: 5)[14].

Persecution leads to Glory

David and the prophets predicted 'the sufferings of the Messiah *and* the glories that would follow[15]. Christ not only gave an example of living through suffering; His suffering was what was going to remove suffering from the world. His death would conquer the sin that caused death. His persecution would win the salvation of the world. The violence directed to Jesus was the means by which He would bring peace between the Triune God and man.

The Seed of the Woman took the sin of His Bride to Himself and died in order to crush the power of the devil. His suffering had a purpose. He humbly accepted the will of the Father. His death would be a terrible moment of spiritual and physical pain, but Christ knew that His Father would

---

13   Psalm 22: 21 can be translated: '... .from the horns of the oxen You have answered me.'

14   See Luke 23: 46.

15   1 Peter 1: 11

see Him through death. Jesus had lived a sinless life which meant that His death was a righteous sacrifice acceptable to His Father:

> [The Lord] rescued me because he delighted in me.
> The Lord has dealt with me according to my righteousness;
>> according to the cleanness of my hands he has rewarded me.
> For I have kept the ways of the Lord;
>> I am not guilty of turning from my God.
> All his laws are before me;
>> I have not turned away from his decrees.
> I have been blameless before him
>> and have kept myself from sin.
> The Lord has rewarded me according to my righteousness,
>> according to the cleanness of my hands in his sight.
> (Psalm 18: 19-24)

Thus Christ had confidence that His Father would resurrect His body:

> I keep my eyes always on the LORD.
>> With him at my right hand, I shall not be shaken.
> Therefore my heart is glad and my tongue rejoices;
>> my body also will rest secure,
> because you will not abandon me to the realm of the dead,
>> nor will you let your faithful one see decay.
> You make known to me the path of life;
>> you will fill me with joy in your presence,
>> with eternal pleasures at your right hand'
> (Psalm 16: 8-11)[16].

---

16   See Acts 2: 24-32; 13: 35.

Even though the LORD Jesus would walk 'through the valley of the shadow of death', He could say with hope: 'I will fear no evil, for you are with me; your rod and your staff, they comfort me'[17].

Jesus would be brought by His Father through death to eternal life. Thus at the resurrection, the Father would say, 'You are my Son; today I have become your Father' (Psalm 2: 7)[18]. He would declare to the world that His living Son was righteous. And in turn the Son would lead the Church in praise of His Father for resurrecting Him from the dead:

> I will declare your name to my people;
> in the assembly I will praise you.
> You who fear the LORD, praise him!
> All you descendants of Jacob, honour him!
> Revere him, all you descendants of Israel!
> For he has not despised or scorned
> the suffering of the afflicted one;
> he has not hidden his face from him
> but has listened to his cry for help.
> (Psalm 22: 22-24).[19]

Glory followed suffering.

The Ascended King

Not only did David look ahead to the LORD Jesus' resurrection, he saw the risen Christ ascending to be with His Father in heaven:

---

17 Psalm 23: 4 (using footnote)

18 See Acts 13: 33, Hebrews 1: 5

19 See Hebrews 2: 12; Psalm 34: 20 cf John 19: 36; Psalm 18: 46-50 cf Romans 15: 9; Psalm 91 cf Luke 4: 11 and 10: 19

Who may ascend the mountain of the LORD?
   Who may stand in his holy place?
The one who has clean hands and a pure heart,
   who does not trust in an idol
   or swear by a false god.
(Psalm 24: 3-4)

The sinless One who had conquered sin and death through His atoning death – the One who had been raised from the dead and given a new righteous life – the One who has 'clean hands and a pure heart' – He would be able to ascend the mountain of the LORD and enter the Most Holy Place.

Lift up your heads, you gates;
   be lifted up, you ancient doors,
   that the King of glory may come in.
Who is this King of glory?
   The LORD strong and mighty,
   the LORD mighty in battle.
Lift up your heads, you gates;
   lift them up, you ancient doors,
   that the King of glory may come in.
Who is he, this King of glory?
   The LORD Almighty –
   he is the King of glory.
(Psalm 24: 7-10)

Christ the King of Glory would enter the presence of His Father. A human being would be welcomed into heaven and sit at the right hand of God Most High. Jesus' death and resurrection would enable God and man to be re-united. David saw ahead to the moment his LORD, the LORD Jesus Christ, would enter heaven and he prophesied:

The LORD says to my Lord:
"Sit at my right hand
until I make your enemies
a footstool for your feet."
The LORD will extend your mighty sceptre from Zion,
saying,
"Rule in the midst of your enemies!"'
(Psalm 110:1-2).[20]

The crucified Christ would rule over the whole universe:

The stone the builders rejected
has become the cornerstone
(Psalm 118:22)[21]

And so in Psalm 22, having foretold the suffering of Christ, David prophesies His authority over the world, now and forever in His glorious new creation:

From you comes the theme of my praise in the great
assembly;
    before those who fear you I will fulfil my vows.
The poor will eat and be satisfied;
    those who seek the LORD will praise him –
    may your hearts live for ever!
All the ends of the earth
    will remember and turn to the LORD,
and all the families of the nations
    will bow down before him,
for dominion belongs to the LORD
    and he rules over the nations.
All the rich of the earth will feast and worship;
    all who go down to the dust will kneel before him –
    those who cannot keep themselves alive.

---

20   Matthew 22: 44; Acts 2: 34-35; Hebrews 1: 13.
21   See Luke 20: 17, Acts 4: 11, 1 Peter 2:7.

Posterity will serve him;

future generations will be told about the Lord.

They will proclaim his righteousness,

declaring to a people yet unborn:

He has done it!

(Psalm 22: 25-31)

David the persecuted

David saw what was ahead in relation to Christ's work of salvation, and prophesied about His life, death, resurrection, ascension and His return in glory to institute the new creation. And within these prophecies, David recorded the LORD Jesus' prayers of dependency on His Father in the light of His suffering.

So how did this knowledge of Christ's suffering and glory help David as he was being hunted down by Saul and his army? How did the Psalms help him? The answers are unpacked below:

First, David knew that because he trusted in Christ's work of salvation, he could relate to the Triune God. David testified that the Lord Jesus was '**my** LORD' (Psalm 110: 1). Through his faith in Christ, David was united to His death, resurrection and ascension. He had been brought into the Divine Family; he was saved from his sin and death; was counted as blameless before the true and living God. Thus David could sing:

Blessed is the one

whose transgressions are forgiven,

whose sins are covered.

Blessed is the one

whose sin the LORD does not count against them.

(Psalm 35: 1-2)[22]

---

22 See Romans 4: 7-8.

David knew there was nothing he could do to save himself; the LORD Jesus was his Saviour; and thus there was nothing he could do to lose his salvation. Because of Christ, David did not face his suffering as an enemy of the Triune God but as a friend. Because of Christ, nothing could ever separate him from God the Father.

Second, David knew that, through his faith in Christ, he was able to pray to God Most High. He could pour out his anguish when he was suffering using Christ's words in the Psalms. David saw ahead and viewed a Man – the One with clean hands and a pure heart – seated at the right hand of God the Father. Because of His death and resurrection, the LORD Jesus Christ was able to enter the throne room of heaven. He and His Father were united in perfect fellowship through the Holy Spirit.

And through faith in the LORD Jesus, David was also united in fellowship to the Father. Christ had yet to perform His work of salvation but that did not stop David appropriating by faith the benefits of His Saviour's future work. Through the Christ he prophesied, David could boldly approach the throne of God the Father, despite his sinful heart and deeds. Christ, the Great High Priest, opened the way to the Father, enabling David to pray to Him with confidence. The LORD Jesus invited David to pray with Him with to the Father, using the Psalms that the Spirit had inspired David to write. United to Christ's suffering, David could pray the prayers that Jesus prays in the Psalms when He suffers. He could say Christ's words.

So when David was being hunted by his enemies, he could sing with Christ:

My thoughts trouble me and I am distraught
> because of what my enemy is saying,
> because of the threats of the wicked;
for they bring down suffering on me
> and assail me in their anger.
My heart is in anguish within me;
> the terrors of death have fallen on me.
Fear and trembling have beset me;
> horror has overwhelmed me.
(Psalm 55: 2-5)

As David was under attack, he could identify with the Psalms of Christ's suffering; he *felt* the words of Christ he uttered e.g.:

Dogs surround me,
> a pack of villains encircles me
(Psalm 22:16)

Zeal for your house consumes me,
> and the insults of those who insult you fall on me
(Psalm 69:9).

United to Christ, David could pray with total assurance:

I call out to the LORD,
> and he answers me from his holy mountain.
(Psalm 3:4)

In the morning, LORD, you hear my voice;
> in the morning I lay my requests before you
> and wait expectantly.
(Psalm 5:3)

David did not conceal the pain of his persecution, pretending that all was well. He followed the example of Christ who spoke freely to His Father of His anguish at being persecuted.

When in pain, David poured out his heart to his Maker, his Saviour, and his Friend. He was transparent about his fears and terrors. He knew that His LORD understood his suffering and weakness. David was united to Christ's suffering and Christ was united to his. He knew his tears were noticed by the LORD.[23]

Assured of his relationship with the Father through Christ, David had the confidence to share his deepest concerns with his LORD. There was no need for him to hide the fears of his heart behind a formality of speech; there was no shame in voicing his anger. He spewed out his rawest emotions knowing that they would not undermine his relationship with his LORD; that his LORD wanted to hear about his pain, not merely that 'I'm okay'. So David said:

Evening, morning and noon
I cry out in distress
and he hears my voice
(Psalm 55: 16-17).

David did not merely cry out to the LORD; he *complained* to Him. Not behind His back; but to His face, as a child to their Father. David complained as someone who knew that the LORD is merciful and just, and yet often found himself bewildered at what was happening to him.

How long, Lord? Will you forget me for ever?
How long will you hide your face from me?
How long must I wrestle with my thoughts

---

23 See Psalm 56: 8. This truth about Christ 's oneness with His Church – and the way He cries with His people's cries – is a theme of all the Scriptures. See Isaiah 63: 9. Colossians 1:24-25, 2 Corinthians 1: 5, Ephesians 3: 1, 1 Corinthians 12: 26, 2 Timothy 2: 1-13.

and day after day have sorrow in my heart?
How long will my enemy triumph over me?
Look on me and answer, Lord my God.
    Give light to my eyes, or I will sleep in death,
and my enemy will say, 'I have overcome him,'
    and my foes will rejoice when I fall.'
(Psalm 13: 1-4)

And yet, confident in the love of God, there was always a 'but' after David's cries about his suffering:

But I trust in your unfailing love;
    my heart rejoices in your salvation.
I will sing the LORD's praise,
    for he has been good to me (5-6).

Like Christ, David trusted in the Father; never losing hope when persecuted:

Why, Lord, do you stand far off?
    Why do you hide yourself in times of trouble?
In his arrogance the wicked man hunts down the weak,
 who are caught in the schemes he devises.

But you, God, see the trouble of the afflicted;
    you consider their grief and take it in hand.
The victims commit themselves to you;
    you are the helper of the fatherless.
The Lord is King for ever and ever;
    the nations will perish from his land.
You, Lord, hear the desire of the afflicted;
    you encourage them, and you listen to their cry,
defending the fatherless and the oppressed,
    so that mere earthly mortals
    will never again strike terror.
(Psalm 10: 1-2, 14, 16-18)

Third, David knew that to follow the LORD Jesus Christ was a path that would lead to suffering. David saw ahead the sufferings of Christ. He knew the LORD God as He truly is – not a remote, abstract deity, but the God who sends His Son into the world: the Son who, out of love for humanity, is mocked and rejected.

David knew the opposition the LORD Jesus faced and so knew that as a follower of the LORD, he must also expect opposition. *That was to be like Christ.* Those who follow other gods will look to harm an ambassador of the LORD Jesus. David could echo the cry of another Psalmist who shouted out to Christ Jesus, 'For your sake we face death all day long; we are considered as sheep to be slaughtered' (Psalm 44: 22[24]).

David would not have been surprised therefore that he suffered because of Christ. That did not make it easier for him to experience such persecution; it did not make his suffering any less unjust. But it was something he would have expected to happen; his suffering had meaning; it was part of the privilege and cost of following Christ.

Fourth, because David trusted in Christ's salvation, he had confidence that He ruled over the enemies of His Church <u>now</u>. The prophet looked ahead and saw the risen Christ sitting at the right hand of His Father – death and sin defeated. As he saw Jesus' ascension, David had confidence that his LORD reigned over the whole world and would look after him day by day:

When you ascended on high,
    you took many captives;
    you received gifts from people,

---

24   See Romans 8: 36

even from the rebellious –

that you, LORD God, might dwell there.

Praise be to the Lord, to God our Saviour,

who daily bears our burdens.

(Psalm 68: 18-19)[25].

David trusted in the protection of Christ:

The angel of the Lord encamps around those who fear him,

and he delivers them.

Taste and see that the Lord is good;

blessed is the one who takes refuge in him.

Fear the Lord, you his holy people,

for those who fear him lack nothing.

(Psalm 34: 7-8)

At any time of trouble, David could take heart by singing to himself:

Truly my soul finds rest in God;

my salvation comes from him.

Truly he is my rock and my salvation;

he is my fortress, I shall never be shaken.

(Psalm 62: 1-2)

Fifth, David could put his suffering in an eternal perspective. He looked forward to the Day when all the LORD's enemies would be a footstool (Psalm 110: 1)[26]. He had confidence that:

The Lord reigns for ever;

he has established his throne for judgment.

He rules the world in righteousness

and judges the peoples with equity.

25   See Ephesians 4: 7-10

26   Psalm 8: 4-6

And so:

> The Lord is a refuge for the oppressed,
>> a stronghold in times of trouble.
> Those who know your name trust in you,
>> for you, Lord, have never forsaken those who seek you.
> (Psalm 9:7-10)[27]

David looked forward to the day where there would be no more persecution – when the LORD Jesus would institute the new creation, when all sin and decay and death would be removed from the world. Christ's people must walk in His footsteps: suffering; then glory. And so David echoed the words of the afflicted man writing in Psalm 102:

> Hear my prayer, LORD;
>> let my cry for help come to you...
> In my distress I groan aloud
>> and am reduced to skin and bones...
> All day long my enemies taunt me;
>> those who rail against me use my name as a curse...
> But you, LORD, sit enthroned for ever;
>> your renown endures through all generations...
> He will respond to the prayer of the destitute;
>> he will not despise their plea...
> So the name of the LORD will be declared in Zion
>> and his praise in Jerusalem
> when the peoples and the kingdoms
>> assemble to worship the LORD.
> In the course of my life he broke my strength;
>> he cut short my days.

---

27 The Psalm is – appropriately – sung to the tune of 'Death of the Son'. David had confidence in Christ's power over his enemies because Christ's death would conquer sin, the devil and death.

So I said:

    'Do not take me away, my God, in the midst of my days;

    your years go on through all generations.

In the beginning you laid the foundations of the earth,

    and the heavens are the work of your hands.

They will perish, but you remain;

    they will all wear out like a garment.

Like clothing you will change them

    and they will be discarded.

But you remain the same,

    and your years will never end.

The children of your servants will live in your presence;

    their descendants will be established before you.'

(Psalm 102: 1, 5, 8, 12, 17, 21-28)[28]

David knew the LORD was the true King of Israel, ruling over the universe. Thus he did not need to fear his enemies. Nor did he need to bring justice on them when they attacked him: that could be left to the LORD Jesus:

The righteous will be glad when they are avenged,

    when they dip their feet in the blood of the wicked.

Then people will say,

 'Surely the righteous still are rewarded;

 surely there is a God who judges the earth.'

(Psalm 58: 10-11)

Do not fret because of those who are evil

    or be envious of those who do wrong;

for like the grass they will soon wither,

    like green plants they will soon die away.

---

28   See Hebrews 1: 10-12

Trust in the Lord and do good;
    dwell in the land and enjoy safe pasture.
Take delight in the Lord,
    and he will give you the desires of your heart.

Commit your way to the Lord;
    trust in him and he will do this:
he will make your righteous reward shine like the dawn,
    your vindication like the noonday sun.

Be still before the LORD
    and wait patiently for him;
do not fret when people succeed in their ways,
    when they carry out their wicked schemes.

Refrain from anger and turn from wrath;
    do not fret—it leads only to evil.
For those who are evil will be destroyed,
    but those who hope in the LORD will inherit the
land.

A little while, and the wicked will be no more;
    though you look for them, they will not be found.
But the meek will inherit the land
    and enjoy peace and prosperity.

The wicked plot against the righteous
    and gnash their teeth at them;
but the Lord laughs at the wicked,
    for he knows their day is coming.
(Psalm 37: 1-13)[29]

David endured his persecution knowing that LORD would judge his enemies: they would be punished for their

---

29   See also Psalm 9: 11-20.

wickedness – either in his lifetime or when Christ returned from heaven to judge the wicked and remove them from the earth. David had learnt from Moses the words of the LORD: 'It is mine to avenge; I will repay'[30]. David could leave the judgement of his persecutors to his LORD. His duty was to repay evil with good not evil:

> Whoever of you loves life
>   and desires to see many good days,
> keep your tongue from evil
>   and your lips from telling lies.
> Turn from evil and do good;
> seek peace and pursue it.
>
> The eyes of the Lord are on the righteous,
>   and his ears are attentive to their cry;
> but the face of the Lord is against those who do evil,
>   to blot out their name from the earth.
> (Psalm 34: 12-16)[31]

Knowing that the LORD would ultimately clear away all His enemies from the world and make the creation new did not diminish the pain David experienced at the hands of Saul and others. Yet he knew in his head and his heart that the LORD Jesus reigned; that his suffering was temporary; that a glorious future awaited him and all the saints. There were many times when David did not know why the Triune God was inflicting suffering on him and he cried out 'Why?'. Yet in his pain he trusted ever more deeply in what he did know about his LORD: in His goodness, His power, and His

---

30   Deut. 32:35 cf Romans 12: 17-21

31   See 1 Peter 3: 8-15. David showed this gracious attitude to his enemies when he chose not to take Saul's life when he had the opportunity, having been hunted down by the king and his men (1 Samuel 24 and 26).
See also Psalm 141: 4, Psalm 7: 1-5.

salvation of His people from sin and death. David had confidence that the LORD was sovereign over all, and so David could cling on to Him when others were against him:

> I cry aloud to the Lord;
>> I lift up my voice to the Lord for mercy.
> I pour out before him my complaint;
>> before him I tell my trouble.
> When my spirit grows faint within me,
>> it is you who watch over my way.
> In the path where I walk
>> people have hidden a snare for me.
> Look and see, there is no one at my right hand;
>> no one is concerned for me.
> I have no refuge;
>> no one cares for my life.
> I cry to you, Lord;
>> I say, 'You are my refuge,
> my portion in the land of the living.
> (Psalm 142: 1-5)

Singing the Psalms

With faith in Christ, David found comfort in the Psalms when suffering at the hands of his enemies. And the LORD Jesus invites all His followers to pray with Him the prayers He prayed when facing His persecution.

The 150 Psalms in the Scriptures provide a wonderful testimony to the LORD Jesus Christ and His work of salvation. They are written so the Church might learn of the way He was persecuted and the glories that followed, and how, in the light of His work of salvation, the Church can endure the persecution which the followers of Christ must expect. The Psalms were written for the Church in all ages that they follow the example of Christ's dependency on God the Father:

> Let this be written for a future generation,
>> that a people not yet created may praise the LORD:
> 'The LORD looked down from his sanctuary on high,
>> from heaven he viewed the earth,
> to hear the groans of the prisoners
>> and release those condemned to death.'
> So the name of the LORD will be declared in Zion
>> and his praise in Jerusalem
> when the peoples and the kingdoms
>> assemble to worship the LORD.
> (Psalm 102: 18-22)[32]

For all those Christians who suffer, the Psalms offer rich words of comfort by pointing us to the LORD Jesus Christ, who faced His suffering with complete trust in His Father, His strength and refuge. 'So we say with confidence'[33]:

> The Lord is with me; I will not be afraid.
>> What can mere mortals do to me? (Psalm 118:6-7)

---

32 See Psalm 22: 29-31. The Holy Spirit testifies elsewhere in the Scriptures of the Christ-centred focus of the Psalms – see Luke 24: 44-47; Colossians 3: 15-17, Ephesians 5: 18-20.

33 Hebrews 13: 6

CHAPTER SIX

WHEN THE KING CONTROLS RELIGION

Imagine this situation. A woman sits in jail. Her crime? She was caught giving a Bible to a neighbour. That is illegal in the land in which she dwells. The government has made it an offence to publish or circulate any material promoting a religion other than the one sanctioned by the state. The government – run by a nationalist, avowedly secular political party – has made it the law that there is only one official religion. Those not of that religion are effectively second-class citizens, with fewer rights than those of the majority religion. All the adherents of the official religion are encouraged by their leaders to vote for the governing party. They are banned from converting to Christianity.

The woman has not been allowed any visitors; there is no word yet on when her case will be heard. But while she is in jail, she is able to witness to her fellow inmates, many of whom become Christians. The government's attempt to stamp out the name of Christ leads to more people being drawn to Him.

It does not take much imagination to think of a story like this for similar events are happening all over the world today and have occurred in every generation. The Bible speaks to such situations through its stories of kings forbidding Christ's name being proclaimed. This chapter studies one such ruler, Jeroboam, the king of Israel. The Bible passage is 1 Kings 12 and 13.

From David to Jeroboam

After Saul died, David became the ruler of Israel. He was promised that Christ would be one of his descendants[1], and that, as a sign of that prophecy, his natural offspring would rule on the throne as long as they remained faithful to the LORD.[2]

David was first succeeded by his son. Solomon. Initially faithful, Solomon turned away from the LORD Jesus to serve other gods and as judgment the Triune God promised that He would tear the kingdom out of Solomon's hand and give most of the tribes of Israel to one of his officials – Jeroboam, who had rebelled against the king (1 Kings 12: 31). But, the LORD promised that He would leave one of David's descendants to rule the tribe of Judah – 'for the sake of my servant David and the city of Jerusalem, which I have chosen out of all the tribes of Israel' (1 Kings 11: 32).

Solomon's son, Rehoboam, became king of Judah. Jeroboam became king of the northern kingdom of Israel.

Jeroboam's sin

Jeroboam did not see the hand of the Triune God elevating him to power. He believed he gained the kingship through his own political will. And he paid no heed to God the Father, Son and Holy Spirit when on the throne in Israel. His focus was on cementing his political power:

Jeroboam fortified Shechem in the hill country of Ephraim and lived there. From there he went out and built up Peniel.

1   2 Samuel 7: 8-16.

2   1 Kings 2: 4

> Jeroboam thought to himself, 'The kingdom is now likely to revert to the house of David. If these people go up to offer sacrifices at the temple of the LORD in Jerusalem, they will again give their allegiance to their lord, Rehoboam king of Judah. They will kill me and return to King Rehoboam.'
>
> After seeking advice, the king made two golden calves. He said to the people, 'It is too much for you to go up to Jerusalem. Here are your gods, Israel, who brought you up out of Egypt.' One he set up in Bethel, and the other in Dan. And this thing became a sin; the people came to worship the one at Bethel and went as far as Dan to worship the other.
>
> Jeroboam built shrines on high places and appointed priests from all sorts of people, even though they were not Levites. He instituted a festival on the fifteenth day of the eighth month, like the festival held in Judah, and offered sacrifices on the altar. This he did in Bethel, sacrificing to the calves he had made. And at Bethel he also installed priests at the high places he had made. On the fifteenth day of the eighth month, a month of his own choosing, he offered sacrifices on the altar he had built at Bethel. So he instituted the festival for the Israelites and went up to the altar to make offerings. (1 Kings 12: 25-33).

Jerusalem was the place where the LORD had commanded the people to gather to bring their sacrifices in the Promised Land. The LORD had specifically told the ancient Church that there was to be *one* place of worship – the place where the LORD above would put His Name.[3] Jerusalem was the place where the Messiah was going to be sacrificed for the

---

3   See Deuteronomy 12.

sins of the world.[4] The Israelites were to bring to that city the sacrifices which pointed forward to the Messiah, and to have fellowship there with the pre-incarnate LORD Jesus. To bring the sacrifices to a place other than Jerusalem was to seek salvation away from the LORD.

Yet that was what Jeroboam forced the Israelites to do. He created different places of worship – Bethel and Dan – to which they had to bring their sacrifices. And – also contrary to the Law of Moses – he appointed his own priests to carry out these sacrifices.

All this he did for political reasons.

Throughout his reign, Saul was torn between his faith in the LORD and his concern for his political power. Jeroboam's agenda was solely about his own power: that was his god. He did not want the people to travel to the temple in Jerusalem because he was scared that he would lose their allegiance. They might defect to the southern kingdom and leave him without a people to rule. 'A large population is a king's glory, but without subjects a prince is ruined' (Proverbs 14: 28).

The laws given to Israel about sacrifices and priests represented a practical political difficulty for Jeroboam: one which he sought to solve by creating his own sacrificial system, with his own priests, even his own gods in the form of the two golden calves.[5] He did not understand the

---

4   Abraham had been told in Genesis 22 that the Sacrifice of the Lamb would be provided on Mount Moriah – the mountain of the LORD – on which Jerusalem was built (2 Chronicles 3: 1).

5   Following Aaron's bad example, Jeroboam claimed that it was the golden calves which brought Israel out of Egypt and not the Angel of the LORD – the LORD Jesus Christ (1 Kings 12: 28 cf Exodus 32: 1-8). One could hardly credit that the Israelites should believe such nonsense if it wasn't for all the nonsense that any of us believe when we don't trust in the LORD Jesus.

Christological significance of the Law of Moses. He could not see Christ in the sacrifices; he did not see that those sacrifices showed the people the nature of their true Divine King. He was blind to the testimony of the Law that the true King was to sacrifice **Himself** in order to atone for the sins of humanity and reconcile them to God the Father. The sacrifices of the Law showed that the true King served other people not Himself.

Yet Israel's king was only focused on his own agenda. His heart was obsessed with his own power: the need to be in charge; to rule over others; to make them do his will; to honour and obey him.

A Word of Judgment

Jeroboam had no interest in Jesus and His work of salvation. He was prepared to allow his people freedom to worship as long as that did not undermine his power: religion, along with everything else in the land, had to be under his control. God was subject to him. Or so he thought. He did not know what was coming next:

> By the word of the LORD a man of God came from Judah to Bethel, as Jeroboam was standing by the altar to make an offering. (1 Kings 13: 1).

A man of God – a prophet – was sent to Jeroboam. He was sent by the Word of the LORD: the Word who was God and was with God in the beginning.[6] The Triune God was not blind to the way that Jeroboam was enticing the people of Israel away from the LORD Jesus Christ in order to cement his own power and authority. And so the LORD in heaven sent His Word to commission the man of God to go and confront the king.

---

6   John 1: 1-2.

We know little about the anonymous prophet; but it must have taken great courage for him to fulfil his task. He would have known that to challenge the king was to put his life in danger. As noted in a previous chapter, sometimes persecution simply engulfs followers of Christ (as it did with the priests of Nob); they just happen to be standing in the wrong place at the wrong time. In other situations, Christians know there is a strong likelihood of their being persecuted if they witness to Christ to the people around them. Elsewhere disciples of the LORD Jesus are called by the Triune God to do things which they know will inevitably result in their persecution. And so it was with the man of God as he went off to face Jeroboam. Truly he feared God not man. Just how much are we prepared to give up for the sake of Jesus? A little bit of our time? A small amount of our money and possessions? But what about our whole life? Is Jesus that important to us?

As the prophet approached Jeroboam, the king was making an offering at one of the altars he had created at Bethel, as though he himself was priest. The man of God must have been outraged at the sight; yet he must have trembled also as he saw Israel's ruler. Perhaps he sang some Psalms to keep himself focused on the Man of God – the Suffering Servant. *'The Lord is with me; I will not be afraid. What can mere mortals do to me?'* (Psalm 118: 6).

And then the prophet spoke boldly the message the Word of the LORD had given him:

> By the word of the LORD he cried out against the altar: 'Altar, altar! This is what the LORD says: 'A son named Josiah will be born to the house of David. On you he will sacrifice the priests of the high places who make

offerings here, and human bones will be burned on you.'
That same day the man of God gave a sign: 'This is the
sign the LORD has declared: the altar will be split apart
and the ashes on it will be poured out.' (1 Kings 13: 2-3).

The prophet did not even speak to the king; it was as though
he was irrelevant. It was the altar which the man of God
addressed. The altar was supposed to focus the people on
Christ. His body would be sacrificed on the altar to make
atonement for them. The altar was a precious, precious
symbol of Christ and His sacrifice. Yet here it was being
used by Israel's false priests to make their false sacrifices to
maintain Jeroboam's political rule.

No wonder the man of God cried out against its
blasphemy. He cursed it. And the prophet saw ahead to a
time when a descendent of David, Josiah, would sacrifice
the idolatrous priests upon it. No longer would the priests
bring their worthless sacrifices to the altar; they would be
the ones burnt upon it. The prophecy could not be clearer:
without Jesus, the priests had nothing to save themselves
from the flames on the altar. Their fate would be the fate of
all those who reject Jesus. Reject Christ's sacrifice and you
will be sacrificed yourself. Reject Christ and you have
nothing to protect you from the wrath of the Triune God.

Seize him!

By not even speaking to Jeroboam, the man of God signalled
the king's insignificance. The prophet's concern was with
the reformation of the Church: that Israel should be Israel;
living according to the Law of Moses with the priests
performing sacrifices at Jerusalem to build people up in

their faith in Christ. Only by living for the LORD could Israel fulfil its task to be His ambassadors to the nations around them. Israel was supposed to be living by grace: loving their neighbours, seeking justice, caring for the poor, looking after their animals and the land.

The prophet had been sent by the Word of the LORD to proclaim that He was King: that He ruled over Israel; that the kingdom of Jesus was not to be controlled by human rulers.

Here was an opportunity for Jeroboam to grasp salvation: to clutch at eternal life in the face of the prophecy of death. But the king did not want to be a subject of Christ's kingdom. He wanted to rule his own. He did not tolerate anyone who did not wish to follow the state religion he had created. Such a person was disloyal. Jeroboam could not bear even to hear a word against the state religion:

> When King Jeroboam heard what the man of God cried out against the altar at Bethel, he stretched out his hand from the altar and said, 'Seize him!' (1 Kings 13: 4)

Suddenly the war against Christ was dramatically revealed. He is the Rock on which all gods, power and authorities stumble. There is no neutral spiritual position – people are either for Jesus or against Him. Those who build their own gods will do anything to protect them against Christ. They lash out in violence against Him and His followers. They cannot bear any threat to their religion. Hence why Jeroboam ordered the man of God should be seized. He must be silenced; imprisoned. Jesus and His followers must be eliminated.

Matthew Henry comments on Jeroboam's folly:

> Instead of trembling at the message, as he might well have done, he assaulted him that brought it, in defiance of the wrath of which he was warned and contempt of that grace which sent him the warning. Rebuke a sinner and he will hate thee, and do thee a mischief if he can.[7]

Yet the true and living God protected His prophet from the king:

> ...the hand he stretched out towards the man shrivelled up, so that he could not pull it back. Also, the altar was split apart and its ashes poured out according to the sign given by the man of God by the word of the LORD (1 Kings 13: 4-5).

In every generation, the Triune God works miracles to protect His people. The lack of feeling in his hand made even the king recognise that some special power was at work, thwarting his attempt to overcome the prophet by force. But the king remained in type: he sought a political solution to the 'problem' of God – by seeking to negotiate with Him:

> The king said to the man of God, 'Intercede with the LORD your God and pray for me that my hand may be restored.' (1 Kings 13: 6).

It's amusing to note that at this time of trouble Jeroboam did not call on the two golden calves he had made. Nor did he get the priests he had instituted to burn offerings on his behalf. Instead he turned to the man he had just persecuted – in order that he might turn to his LORD for help. This was a crisis: the king didn't bother with any of the religion he had

---

7   Matthew Henry, op cit, 500

created. He knew it had no power. He needed something he thought would work. When times are desperate even the most pagan people turn to Christians for help[8].

But note also that the king did not ask that his sins be taken away; that his evil heart might be cured; that he might relate to the true and living God. He merely wanted his hand to be healed.

Hearing the king's request, the prophet may have been tempted to curse him rather than intercede with the LORD but the man of God followed the way of Christ set out in the law of Moses: Do not seek revenge or bear a grudge against anyone among your people but love your neighbour as yourself (Leviticus 19: 18)[9]. The prophet prayed for the king:

> So the man of God interceded with the LORD, and the
> king's hand was restored and became as it was before
> (1 Kings 13: 6).

The prophet could do what the king could not – he could relate to the Holy Almighty God. Why? Because of Jesus his Great Priest. Through Jesus he could access heaven itself and speak to God Most High. And his prayer was answered. The king's hand was restored. But his heart remained cut off from the LORD. He did not fall on his knees repenting of his sin. He remained focused on the maintenance of his political authority. And he calculated that if could not crush the man of God, he needed to get him on side:

---

8   Later, when his son becomes ill, Jeroboam again turns to a prophet for help (1 Kings 14). For another example, see how Pharaoh sought Moses' help to take away the plagues that fell on Egypt in the book of Exodus, although without ever softening his heart to the Triune God.

9   Matthew 5: 44-45: Love your enemies and pray for those who persecute you, that you may be children of your Father in heaven.

The king said to the man of God, 'Come home with me for a meal, and I will give you a gift.' But the man of God answered the king, 'Even if you were to give me half your possessions, I would not go with you, nor would I eat bread or drink water here. For I was commanded by the word of the LORD: "You must not eat bread or drink water or return by the way you came."' So he took another road and did not return by the way he had come to Bethel (1 Kings 13: 7-10).

The king's offer may have seemed a genuine act of gratitude and hospitality but the LORD knew that Jeroboam's real motive for inviting the prophet into his household was to harness the divine power that he was able to wield. The king wanted an alliance. He wanted the prophet to serve the state. If the man of God could not be defeated by violence he must be bribed; tamed; controlled.

The Word of the LORD had foreseen what the king would do and he told the prophet prior to meeting the king – at the time of his commissioning – not to accept any hospitality on his journey. How tempting it must have been for him to join the household of Jeroboam: *Perhaps I could be of influence there; I could offer a prophetic voice to the kingdom; It's vital to speak the truth to political power; I could be salt and light in the king's palace.*

Or the prophet could simply have fancied gaining some money.

But, like Abraham and Moses[10] before him, he rejected the wealth and influence of a king for the sake of Christ – the true Divine King. Christ alone was his LORD: he could not trust in a human ruler as well. It was one or the other. His loyalty was toward Jesus and His Kingdom, not Jeroboam and his.

---

10   Genesis 14: 17-24, Hebrews 11: 26.

The End of Jeroboam

Having turned down the king's offer, the man of God went on his way[11]; and the king returned to his ways. His brief encounter with the God of the prophet appeared to have no lasting influence on him. He had felt the powerlessness in his hand when confronted by the power of the Spirit of the LORD; but he still believed that his strength was greater than that of the God of the prophet. The king rejected his opportunity to reach out to the LORD and find life; and his heart hardened. He closed his ears to the prophecy of the man of God. He had been warned in the clearest terms of what would happen to the altar and the priests who ministered at it. Yet:

> Even after this, Jeroboam did not change his evil ways, but once more appointed priests for the high places from all sorts of people. Anyone who wanted to become a priest he consecrated for the high places. This was the sin of the house of Jeroboam that led to its downfall and to its destruction from the face of the earth (1 Kings 13: 33-34).

Jeroboam paid no heed to the Word of the LORD; he continued to appoint his own priests in order to keep his people away from Jerusalem – away from Jesus. He continued to use the power of the state to control Israel's religion in order to boost his own authority.

---

11   Having resisted the enticements offered by the king, the prophet promptly succumbed to a subtler temptation – 1 Kings 13: 11-32. No doubt he was exhausted by his dealings with Jeroboam and the courage and wisdom he had shown in dealing with the king deserted him. It's a story teaching the followers of Christ to pray constantly not to be lead into temptation. Although the prophet was judged for his sin – he could not be a prophet if he did not obey the Word of the LORD – he was honoured for his faithfulness in denouncing Jeroboam's creation of a false religion to serve his own ends (see 2 Kings 23: 15-18).

In His grace, God Most High sent His Word again to the king: the message going through the prophet Ahijah, via his wife:

'Go, tell Jeroboam that this is what the Lord, the God of Israel, says: "I raised you up from among the people and appointed you ruler over my people Israel. I tore the kingdom away from the house of David and gave it to you, but you have not been like my servant David, who kept my commands and followed me with all his heart, doing only what was right in my eyes. You have done more evil than all who lived before you. You have made for yourself other gods, idols made of metal; you have aroused my anger and turned your back on me.

'"Because of this, I am going to bring disaster on the house of Jeroboam. I will cut off from Jeroboam every last male in Israel – slave or free. I will burn up the house of Jeroboam as one burns dung, until it is all gone. Dogs will eat those belonging to Jeroboam who die in the city, and the birds will feed on those who die in the country. The LORD has spoken!"' (1 Kings 14: 7-11)[12]

There was a prophecy against Israel too because of the sin of Jeroboam.

The Lord will raise up for himself a king over Israel who will cut off the family of Jeroboam. Even now this is beginning to happen. And the Lord will strike Israel, so that it will be like a reed swaying in the water. He will uproot Israel from this good land that he gave to their ancestors and scatter them beyond the River Euphrates, because they aroused the Lord's anger by making

---

12 Out of Jeroboam's household it appears that only his son had a faith in the LORD (1 Kings 14: 12-13).

Asherah poles. And he will give Israel up because of the sins Jeroboam has committed and has caused Israel to commit. (1 Kings 14: 14-16)

The prophet's word gave Jeroboam one more chance to repent; but his heart was hard. He had rejected the Word of the LORD; and now the LORD rejected Jeroboam. There were no more opportunities to turn to the LORD. His fate was final. The king went to his grave alienated from the Triune God[13].

Jeroboam had not believed the Word of the LORD and had sought to go his own way, trusting in his own power. Yet all that the Word said came true: the altar split in two, the king's household was wiped off the face of the earth; the bones of the priests of Bethel were burnt upon the altar; Israel was eventually exiled from the land.[14]

Jeroboam did not go unpunished for the crimes against the LORD and His Church. The Triune God did judge Jeroboam. He is sovereign. He does not allow those who persecute His church to go unpunished; there is a reckoning; an account must be given by those who spill a Christian's blood.

The Triune God will deal with the evil committed against them by their persecutors, whether members of their family, or political or religious authorities or colleagues or neighbours. There are eternal consequences to what people do.

The Continuing Sin of Jeroboam

Despite the LORD's judgement upon Jeroboam, his successors as the kings of Israel did not learn their lesson. The Holy Spirit repeatedly denounces them for following

---

13   1 Kings 14: 20
14   See 1 Kings 13: 5, 1 Kings 15: 27-30, 2 Kings 23: 1-20, 2 Kings 17.

'the sins of Jeroboam' or walking in 'the ways of Jeroboam'[15]. These kings, like Jeroboam, sought to maintain a state religion which was opposed to Jesus in order to uphold their political power. Jacques Ellul, the French theologian, comments as follows:

> The sin of Jeroboam was precisely that he made theological and religious decisions regarding the true God for political reasons, thus subordinating the spiritual life of the people to political necessity, orientating its worship, not to another lord, but according to the demands of politics, seizing control of the revelation of God, playing the role of the prophet in order to distinguish the true God. 'Behold your gods... who brought you out of the land of Egypt' (1 Kings 12: 28). It is thus the state which sets its seal on both the truth of revelation and also the conditions in which the people will hear and worship. But when the state does this, it is for political motives. What we have here, then, is not an idolatrous state but a political power which creates a state religion or which uses the truth of God, the revelation of God, and the work of God for political ends. It subordinates the will of God, not to its own will, but to the greater good of the nation or the state. It integrates God's will into the imperative of a realistic policy.

> The great aim of Jeroboam was the security of the religion of Israel. To achieve this he took the necessary material steps. He built cities and forts, Shechem and Penuel. But he also took spiritual and psychological steps. We see here the intentional and deliberate establishment of a national religion in the service of the

---

15   See 1 Kings 15:34, 1 Kings 16:1-31, 1 Kings 21:22, 1 Kings 22:52, 2 Kings 3:3, 2 Kings 9:9, 2 Kings 10:29, 2 Kings 13:1-11, 2 Kings 14:24, 2 Kings 15:9, 18, 24, 28, 2 Kings 17:21-23, 2 Kings 23:15.

state and for the purpose of unifying national sentiment. There is nothing at all 'primitive' about this. It is just what we all do. Every modern state thinks that it should establish in the same way a full-scale religion which will serve to unite the people and make it loyal to the political power, integrating the church so that it will be 'national' and will fill this same role.

Politics demands religion as an ally.[16]

All political rulers face the temptation to follow the 'sin of Jeroboam' – to demand loyalty to a religion opposed to Jesus.

The Victorious Church

We know from 1 Kings that such rulers will not win. Nevertheless, we might be tempted to think that Jeroboam was reasonably successful in achieving his political aim: of ensuring that his people did not overthrow him and give their allegiance to Rehoboam king of Judah. You might concede that Jeroboam, for all his faults, was an effective politician. However, the Holy Spirit highlights in another part of Scripture that whilst Jeroboam was in power a subversive movement was taking place:

The priests and Levites from all their districts throughout Israel sided with [Rehoboam, king of Judah]. The Levites even abandoned their pasture-lands and property and came to Judah and Jerusalem, because Jeroboam and his sons had rejected them as priests of the LORD when he appointed his own priests for the high places and for the goat and calf idols he had made. Those from every

16   Jacques Ellul, *The Politics of God and the Politics of Man*, William B Eerdmans, Grand Rapids, 1972, 125-126.

tribe of Israel who set their hearts on seeking the LORD, the God of Israel, followed the Levites to Jerusalem to offer sacrifices to the LORD, the God of their ancestors. They strengthened the kingdom of Judah and supported Rehoboam son of Solomon for three years, following the ways of David and Solomon during this time (2 Chronicles 11: 13-17).

How wonderful that as Jeroboam sought to enforce a religion which rejected the LORD Jesus Christ, many of his citizens were flocking to Jerusalem to offer sacrifices at the temple, showing their faith in the Lamb of God. Jeroboam devoted his political life to enforcing a religion which rejected the LORD Jesus Christ. He did all in his power to keep his people from Christ. Yet we read that hundreds, thousands of his citizens flocked to Jerusalem to offer sacrifices at the temple, showing their faith in Christ, their Saviour. The pull of worshipping Jesus was too strong to keep people from Jerusalem. Jeroboam enticed them away from the LORD Jesus; the Holy Spirit moved them to follow Him. Jeroboam sought to frustrate the Church; the LORD carried on building it.

The sin of Jeroboam is the sin that infects so many rulers and governors around the world today. Rather than fulfil their calling to protect the Church and its worship and witness, governments make it illegal for Christians to meet; to evangelise; to own Bibles. They make Christians second class citizens. They fail to step in when adherents of other religions threaten Christians and bully them and torture them and rape them and kill them. And like Jeroboam these rulers look so powerful, so invincible. How can the Church possibly survive against their force?

Yet God the Father, Son and Holy Spirit builds His people. He grows His Church irrespective of what human rulers do to tame or squash it. It is *His* Church not theirs.

Where Christianity is banned, He grows an underground Church so large it can hardly be counted. Where the witness to Jesus seems to have been extinguished in a country, He disperses its people around the world so they can hear the gospel in other countries. Where governments prevent people from accessing the Bible, He gives people dreams of the LORD Jesus. Where face to face evangelism is illegal, He uses the internet and social media to spread the message of Christ.

The movement of the gospel cannot be stopped. The kingdom of God has no borders. The rulers of the world order who and how people may worship. They promote their gods in order to preserve their own power and wealth. They violently force people away from Christ; yet hundreds, thousands, millions are drawn to Him. His beauty cannot be hidden; people are irresistibly attracted to Him – to the beauty of His love, majesty, power, mercy and compassion.

They long to meet their Creator, the Word of the living God. They desire the very Logic of the universe, in whom everything holds together and we find our meaning and purpose. They yearn for the One who came down to earth in human form and became sin for us that we might have eternal life. They are drawn to the One who sacrificed Himself that we might relate to His Holy Father.

'Come to me', He says. 'And find life'. And they come, whatever the obstacles in their way – a vast multitude of them, attracted by the sweetness of His voice. He takes them when they are dirty and tired and wretched and washes away their sins and makes them clean. The Bridegroom dresses His Bride in new clothes. She is lovely to Him; she is the apple of His eye.

When she suffers, He suffers. He protects her. He wipes away her tears. He comforts her. He holds back the arm of those who try to harm her; He judges those who attack her and slander her and imprison her.

More and more people from around the globe are attracted to His loveliness. From every tribe and nation they come to their Lord and Saviour, whatever the kingdoms of the world try to do to stop them and maintain them in darkness. Because they cannot be kept from the Light.

The LORD Jesus is the King of Kings, Lord of Lords. Nothing will stop Him building His Church until the day when He comes again and He will remove the kings and the powers of darkness from the earth and the Church – His Bride – will fill the earth and live in glorious splendour with the Father, Son and Spirit forever.

The LORD reigns. Hallelujah.

CHAPTER SEVEN

WHEN THE KING PROMOTES FALSE RELIGION

Here's another imaginary story. A Christian in one of the world's largest countries awaits surgery after suffering a brain haemorrhage. It was caused by violence against him committed by adherents of the official religion in this area of the country. The police are investigating the matter – not the attack on the man, that is, but the fact that he is a follower of Christ. The state only recognises that the official religion exists. Members of the government are ardent followers of this religion. They are committed to eradicating Christianity from the land – by eradicating all the Christians.

Again, one does need much imagination to conjure up this tale for there are endless such stories happening across the world right now. And the temptation for Christians in those situations is to cry out to God the Father: *Where are You? Do You care? How long are You going to allow this to happen?*

1 Kings 16-18 speaks of the crimes that are committed against the followers of Christ when a king promotes a religion which is opposed to Him. The chapters were written to reassure God's people that He does not ignore the suffering of His people; that His power is far greater than that of the rulers of the nations and their gods.

A King worse than Jeroboam

Many of the kings who followed Jeroboam walked in his ways, even though he and his household had been condemned by the LORD for their sins. Yet then someone even worse came to the throne:

> In the thirty-eighth year of Asa king of Judah, Ahab son of Omri became king of Israel, and he reigned in Samaria over Israel for twenty-two years. Ahab son of Omri did more evil in the eyes of the LORD than any of those before him. He not only considered it trivial to commit the sins of Jeroboam son of Nebat, but he also married Jezebel daughter of Ethbaal king of the Sidonians, and began to serve Baal and worship him. He set up an altar for Baal in the temple of Baal that he built in Samaria. Ahab also made an Asherah pole and did more to arouse the anger of the LORD, the God of Israel, than did all the kings of Israel before him (1 Kings 16: 29-33).

The sin of Jeroboam was to create a religion worshipping false gods for his own political purposes. He controlled the religious practice of the land and enticed the people away from the LORD Jesus Christ. It was a moot point whether he believed in the religion he instituted. The sin of Ahab was that he was sincere about his faith in another god and used his political power to compel others to share it. Ahab was a committed worshipper of Baal. He, along with his wife, Jezebel, used the funds of the state to create an altar for Baal; a temple for him; priests to serve him; even his own prophets. And they used the force of the state to coerce Baal-worship throughout Israel.

No doubt many people needed little persuasion to trust in Baal. They were desperate to believe in something; to trust in some higher power; to find some hope for the lives; some means of satisfying their desire for happiness. Having rejected God the Father, Son and Holy Spirit, they looked for all these things in Baal – who could provide none of them.

Others were probably more indifferent to the charms of Baal but took part in the worship of him out of fear of the king or merely to follow the crowd. Whatever the motives of the people, whoever who was not with Christ was against Him. To worship Baal was to worship the devil[1].

But there were some in Israel who refused to bow the knee to Baal; who loved and obeyed the Triune God, revealed through the LORD Jesus. And they paid a terrible price for their faithfulness:

> After a long time, in the third year, the word of the Lord came to Elijah: 'Go and present yourself to Ahab, and I will send rain on the land.' So Elijah went to present himself to Ahab.
>
> Now the famine was severe in Samaria, and Ahab had summoned Obadiah, his palace administrator. (Obadiah was a devout believer in the LORD. While Jezebel was killing off the LORD's prophets, Obadiah had taken a hundred prophets and hidden them in two caves, fifty in each, and had supplied them with food and water.) Ahab had said to Obadiah, 'Go through the land to all the springs and valleys. Maybe we can find some grass to keep the horses and mules alive so we will not have to kill any of our animals.' So they divided the land they were to cover, Ahab going in one direction and Obadiah in another (1 Kings 18: 1-6).

---

1   See 2 Kings 1: 2-3, 6 and Matthew 12: 22-32.

The prophet Elijah had previously sent a message to Ahab that there was to be no rain in Israel as judgement upon his worship of Baal (1 Kings 17: 1). Now in the third year of drought, the land was parched, and Ahab was concerned to find some food for the animals so that they would not need to be killed. How touching. He did not want his animals to die. Yet, we learn, his wife had been 'killing off the LORD's prophets'. The king did not seem so bothered about their deaths.

This was a state-sponsored eradication of the people of the Triune God from the land.

Yet the LORD, the LORD, and the Spirit of the LORD was not silent or passive in the face of this persecution of the prophets. The persecution of His people was the persecution of *Him*. And He acted to uphold His name. He raised up Elijah to issue judgement on Ahab; and He raised up Obadiah right in the heart of Ahab's court in order to help save some of the prophets.

Obadiah's faith

We are told that 'Obadiah was a devout believer in the LORD'. Unlike Moses, who felt compelled to leave Pharaoh's court for the sake of Christ, Obadiah lived out his faith in the LORD Jesus within the centre of Ahab's kingdom – as palace administrator. Perhaps Obadiah had been forced in some way to take the post.[2] Whatever the circumstances, he sought to be faithful to the LORD in his current position of

---

2   It is possible that Obadiah ('Slave of Yahweh') was a Tyrean who came into Israel with Jezebel to administer Ahab's kingdom, but was committed to the old true religion, the religion Solomon had taught to Hiram, the king of Tyre (1 Kings 5). Obadiah refers to the LORD in a similar way to the Sidonian widow (cf 1 Kings 17:12; 18:10) – both of them humbly acknowledging the God of Israel and grateful that He had graciously allowed even them to be part of His Church.

work. Like so many followers of Christ, his calling was to live for his LORD where he was, not run away to somewhere else.

That said, it must have been an extraordinarily difficult position to be in, especially once the king's wife started to butcher the LORD's people. It would have been impossible for Obadiah to be open about his faith at work. Every hour, every day, he needed to calculate what to say; what not to say; how to serve the LORD yet not talk about Him; to try and tell the truth and yet not get himself or others into trouble; to do what he could from his position of influence to save fellow believers knowing he probably could not save them all. One false move and he too would be dead.

Like Solomon[3], Obadiah must have cried to the LORD for wisdom: to have the maturity to discern good from evil; to know whether the means he took were justified by the ends he sought.

> The fear of the Lord is the beginning of wisdom, and knowledge of the Holy One is understanding.
> (Proverbs 9:10)

> Those who trust in themselves are fools, but those who walk in wisdom are kept safe. (Proverbs 28:26)

Every day Obadiah must have faced the temptation to run away; or to give up on the LORD Jesus and worship Baal. Yet he remained faithful and sought to use his position to serve the Church. 'While Jezebel was killing off the Lord's prophets, Obadiah had taken a hundred prophets and hidden them in two caves, fifty in each, and had supplied them with food and water' (1 Kings 18: 4).

---

3   1 Kings 3.

At huge risk to his own life, Obadiah managed to save a hundred lives. Trusting in the Messiah and His sacrifice, he was prepared to risk his own life to keep alive as many of the prophets as he could hide.

Little wonder, therefore, that Obadiah got a bit edgy when Elijah – the most wanted man in Israel – suddenly appeared saying he wanted to see Ahab:

> As Obadiah was walking along, Elijah met him. Obadiah recognised him, bowed down to the ground, and said, 'Is it really you, my lord Elijah?'
>
> 'Yes,' he replied. 'Go tell your master, "Elijah is here."'
>
> 'What have I done wrong,' asked Obadiah, 'that you are handing your servant over to Ahab to be put to death? As surely as the LORD your God lives, there is not a nation or kingdom where my master has not sent someone to look for you. And whenever a nation or kingdom claimed you were not there, he made them swear they could not find you. But now you tell me to go to my master and say, "Elijah is here." I don't know where the Spirit of the LORD may carry you when I leave you. If I go and tell Ahab and he doesn't find you, he will kill me. Yet I your servant have worshipped the LORD since my youth. Haven't you heard, my lord, what I did while Jezebel was killing the prophets of the LORD? I hid a hundred of the Lord's prophets in two caves, fifty in each, and supplied them with food and water. And now you tell me to go to my master and say, "Elijah is here." He will kill me!' Elijah said, 'As the LORD Almighty lives, whom I serve, I will surely present myself to Ahab today.' So Obadiah went to meet Ahab and told him, and Ahab went to meet Elijah. (1 Kings 18: 7-16)

Both Elijah and Obadiah were full of courage; both had their eyes fixed on the LORD Jesus and were looking ahead to their heavenly reward. Yet they had very different callings: one the civil servant, carefully seeking to do God's will through quiet influence in a powerful position; the other the prophet called to speak God's word directly to Israel's king, uttering words of judgement. One in bowler hat and pin-stripes; the other all beard and sandals[4].

Understandably, Obadiah was alarmed at the prospect of Elijah entering the court of Ahab. You can feel the sweat starting to fall from his brow. His delicately-constructed life was going to be put in jeopardy by such a wild and outspoken presence as Elijah. *Why can't he go and be zealous somewhere else? Somewhere which won't get me in trouble? I've worked so hard here to serve the LORD in the best way I can; I don't need Mr Hot Head disturbing it all.*

Meanwhile one can imagine Elijah was growing impatient with Obadiah. *Come on Mr Smoothie. Forget all this diplomatic nonsense. I've no time for your compromises. I'm just going to say it how it is. I'm doing the LORD's work here.*

Different kinds of people with different callings: but one LORD and one Church. Whatever his misgivings, Obadiah accepted that Elijah's mission was from the LORD, and went to tell Ahab that the prophet wanted to see him. All the same, one can imagine that Obadiah was trembling as he approached the king's throne. What Psalm would he have sung? Perhaps Psalm 110 – to feel the reassuring presence of Christ in heaven. 'The Lord says to my Lord: "Sit at my right hand until I make your enemies a footstool for your feet... My Lord is at your right hand, Lord; He will crush kings on the day of his wrath"' (Psalm 110: 1,5).

4   2 Kings 1: 7-8

Perhaps Elijah was also repeating that Scripture to himself. One cannot assume that he felt no fear as he approached Ahab. He, like Obadiah, must have known that his life was in danger as he went to confront the king about the false worship he was promoting in the land. The king had all the power of the state at its disposal: one word and he could have the prophet locked up or executed. Elijah had no human power to keep him safe. He needed to rely totally on God the Father, Son and Holy Spirit.

Elijah holds a competition

Unsurprisingly Ahab wasn't overjoyed to see Elijah:

> He said to him, "Is that you, you troubler of Israel?"
> "I have not made trouble for Israel," Elijah replied. "But you and your father's family have. You have abandoned the Lord's commands and have followed the Baals. Now summon the people from all over Israel to meet me on Mount Carmel. And bring the four hundred and fifty prophets of Baal and the four hundred prophets of Asherah, who eat at Jezebel's table." So Ahab sent word throughout all Israel and assembled the prophets on Mount Carmel. (1 Kings 18: 17-20)

The people were invited to Mount Carmel to witness a showdown between the LORD and Baal. The LORD in heaven could no longer bear to see His people suffer; to witness the violence in the name of Baal against His prophets.

Possibly there were some in the land who thought this clash was rather ludicrous: surely both Elijah and Ahab believed in 'God'. What was the fuss about? Didn't Elijah – and Abraham, Isaac, Jacob and David – believe in the same God as Ahab and his wife?

Yet Elijah made clear to the people they faced a choice: 'How long will you waver between two opinions? If the LORD is God, follow him; but if Baal is God, follow him' (v 21). The purpose of the showdown on Mount Carmel was to demonstrate to the people the identity of the true God – that they could only know God if they knew Christ: the Suffering Servant of the Father, empowered by the Spirit. They had to know about Christ's suffering if they were to know the true and living God. So Elijah said to the people:

> "I am the only one of the Lord's prophets left, but Baal has four hundred and fifty prophets. Get two bulls for us. Let Baal's prophets choose one for themselves, and let them cut it into pieces and put it on the wood but not set fire to it. I will prepare the other bull and put it on the wood but not set fire to it. Then you call on the name of your god, and I will call on the name of the Lord. The god who answers by fire – he is God." (1 Kings 18: 22-24)

Again, to some Israelites this may have seemed a rather bizarre competition – comparable with cheese rolling or toe wrestling. But Elijah was staging it deliberately to reveal the LORD Jesus Christ to Ahab and the people. It would show that power and glory lay not in Baal – and his political backers – but in the sacrifice of the Messiah. It looked as though Baal had triumphed in Israel. As Elijah said, he was the only prophet of the LORD left – the others had been murdered or were in hiding (and so officially did not exist). The prophets of Baal created by the king and his wife far out-numbered the prophets of the LORD. Elijah seemed all alone. Baal appeared to be Almighty – able to provide salvation for the people. But when it came to the test Elijah had set, he was shown to be powerless:

> They called on the name of Baal from morning till noon. 'Baal, answer us!' they shouted. But there was no response; no one answered. And they danced around the altar they had made.
>
> At noon Elijah began to taunt them. 'Shout louder!' he said. 'Surely he is a god! Perhaps he is deep in thought, or busy, or travelling. Maybe he is sleeping and must be awakened.' So they shouted louder and slashed themselves with swords and spears, as was their custom, until their blood flowed. Midday passed, and they continued their frantic prophesying until the time for the evening sacrifice. But there was no response, no one answered, no one paid attention.
> (1 Kings 18: 26-29)

Baal was revealed as a failure. It was then the turn of Elijah – or rather the turn of the LORD Jesus. Elijah summoned the people to stand around him; took 'twelve stones, one for each of the tribes descended from Jacob' (v30). Then with the stones,

> He built an altar in the name of the Lord, and he dug a trench round it large enough to hold two seahs of seed. He arranged the wood, cut the bull into pieces and laid it on the wood. (1 Kings 18: 32-33)

The sacrifice was placed upon the wood surrounded by the stones, thus demonstrating the intimate connection between Christ and His Church. His Sacrifice was for them. Elijah then instructed the people to pour water on the offering and the wood[5]; and:

> At the time of [the evening] sacrifice, the prophet Elijah stepped forward and prayed: 'Lord, the God of Abraham, Isaac and Israel, let it be known today that you are God in Israel and that I am your servant and have done all these things at your command.
>
> Answer me, Lord, answer me, so these people will know that you, Lord, are God, and that you are turning their hearts back again.' (1 Kings 18: 36-37)

It was not mere happenstance that Elijah prayed at the time of the evening sacrifice[6]:

> Something deeper, something more precious was denoted by Elijah's waiting until that particular time. That 'evening sacrifice' which was offered every day in the temple of Jerusalem, three hours before sunset, pointed forward to the antitypical burnt offering, which was to be slain when the fullness of time should come. Relying on that great sacrifice for the sins of God's people which the Messiah would offer at His appearing on earth, His servant now took his place by an altar which pointed forward to the Cross. Elijah, as well as

---

5   In human terms, the pouring of water on the sacrifice made it more difficult, impossible in fact, for the fire to consume it. There could be no doubt in the minds of the Israelites that this was the power of God not some natural conflagration or human trick. Yet was it the water which made the difference? Were the Israelites to note that only a water-drenched sacrifice could absorb the fire from the LORD in heaven? In suggesting the answer is 'yes' to those questions, it is relevant to note that it is after Elijah's sacrifice that the land and the people are blessed by water falling on them (1 Kings 18: 41). Prior to that, water – the sign of the Spirit – had been withheld from the people. Elijah and the widow of Sidon had been blessed by another sign of the Spirit – oil – until the day the LORD sent the rain on Israel (1 Kings 17: 7-14).

6   At the evening sacrifice each day, the ancient Church fed on Christ by sacrificing a lamb, pouring out wine and offering oil-soaked bread (Numbers 28: 1-8). It reminded them of the Lamb of God, whose Spirit-soaked body would shed His blood for their salvation.

> Moses, had an intense interest in that great sacrifice, as was clear from the fact that they "spake of His decease which He should accomplish at Jerusalem" when they appeared and talked with Christ on the mount of transfiguration, Luke 9. 30, 31. It was his faith depending upon, not the blood of a bullock, but the blood of Christ, that Elijah now presented his petitions unto God.'[7]

Trusting in the blood of Christ, Elijah prayed to God Most High and at that moment,

> The fire of the Lord fell and burned up the sacrifice, the wood, the stones and the soil, and also licked up the water in the trench. (1 Kings 18: 38)

Elijah's offering – which had been so carefully arranged to represent the Sacrifice of Christ – was consumed by the fire of the LORD. It vividly showed that Christ alone was fit to deal with the anger of God the Father, Son and Holy Spirit against the sin of humanity. Only His death and resurrection could bring life with the Triune God. Such was the love that the Father and the Spirit had for humanity they were prepared for the Son to be sacrificed for His Bride.

Elijah had unmasked the nakedness of Baal. In the face of the Triune God's anger against sin the idol did nothing; said nothing. Baal was powerless to save the people. His prophets could have called on him for a thousand years and he would not have been able to provide an answer to the problem of God's wrath upon them. Only Christ provided the solution. The efficacy of Elijah's sacrifice revealed the atoning power of the Messiah – that there is a Mediator between God and man – God Himself – the LORD Jesus

---

7   A W Pink, *The Life of Elijah,* The Banner of Truth Trust, London 1963, 150.

Christ, the Great High Priest. Thus, the people finally recognised the identity of the true God:

> 'They fell prostrate and cried, 'The Lord – he is God! The Lord – he is God!' (1 Kings 18: 39).

All the people confessed that the LORD is God. Were they all saved at this point? Whilst it's not entirely clear, we can be confident that the Spirit came upon many and gave them faith in the LORD Jesus to whom they testified.

Ahab and Jezebel had used all the force at their disposal to eradicate God's people, and advance the worship of Baal. Yet their power was completely overturned by Elijah's sign of the Messiah's atoning sacrifice. The suffering and death of the Messiah were more powerful than the sword of the king. The political and religious gods sought to destroy the Messiah and His Church; and yet the death of the Messiah was shown to be the very act which would destroy the power of the political and religious gods and save the Church. 'The stone the builders rejected has become the cornerstone' (Psalm 118: 22). His Sacrifice would triumph over all powers and authorities.[8]

Those without faith in the Messiah had no hiding place from the wrath of God. His fiery anger would descend upon them, as Elijah demonstrated by commanding that the prophets of Baal should be destroyed (v40)[9].

Justice upheld

Ahab and Jezebel, the chief architects of the persecution, remained unrepentant; still believing that they could prevail

---

8   Colossians 2: 13-15.

9   In doing so, Elijah and the people followed the commands of the Law of Moses set out in Deuteronomy 13: 1-11.

over the LORD and His Church by the power of the sword:

> Ahab told Jezebel everything Elijah had done and how he
> had killed all the prophets with the sword. So Jezebel sent
> a messenger to Elijah to say, 'May the gods deal with me,
> be it ever so severely, if by this time tomorrow I do not
> make your life like that of one of them' (1 Kings 19: 1-2).

Having faced enormous courage in confronting Ahab on
Carmel, Elijah was at this point struck by fear and self-pity
(vv3-4). No doubt he was tired from his ordeal; yet rather
than rely on God's strength more in his weakness, he
seemed to depend on Him less. In His grace, the LORD of
heaven sent His Angel to minister to the prophet (vv 5-8).
Elijah was worn down by persecution of the Church, yet the
Angel reminded him that it could not be defeated by a sinful
king. The Eternal God was not to be beaten by temporary
wickedness.

> '[Elijah said], 'I have been very zealous for the LORD
> God Almighty. The Israelites have rejected your
> covenant, torn down your altars, and put your prophets
> to death with the sword. I am the only one left, and now
> they are trying to kill me too.'
>
> The LORD said to him, 'Go back the way you came, and
> go to the Desert of Damascus. When you get there,
> anoint Hazael king over Aram. Also, anoint Jehu son of
> Nimshi king over Israel, and anoint Elisha son of Shaphat
> from Abel Meholah to succeed you as prophet. Jehu will
> put to death any who escape the sword of Hazael, and
> Elisha will put to death any who escape the sword of
> Jehu. Yet I reserve seven thousand in Israel – all whose
> knees have not bowed down to Baal and whose mouths
> have not kissed him' (1 Kings 19: 14-18).

However much the king tried to promote his false religion; however much he used the power of the state to outlaw anyone worshipping the true God; the LORD could not be defeated. Christ could not be overcome. He continued to build His Church; He continued to protect and nourish all those who kissed the Son[10] not Baal.

As a sign of His protection of His people the LORD had Ahab and Jezebel put to death; all their power was removed from in an instant; even their memory was removed from the land. He was in control; He had always been sovereign over their plans, as He was sovereign over Ahab's successors. He anointed a new king and gave him the commission:

> You are to destroy the house of Ahab your master, and **I will avenge the blood of my servants the prophets and the blood of all the LORD's servants shed by Jezebel.** The whole house of Ahab will perish. I will cut off from Ahab every last male in Israel – slave or free… As for Jezebel, dogs will devour her on the plot of ground at Jezreel, and no one will bury her (2 Kings 9: 6-10)[11].

The LORD avenged the blood of His prophets which had been shed by Ahab and Jezebel. The LORD vanquished their evil. Nothing was left of them; their household was wiped out. They were completely removed from the land.

The LORD would not allow that evil to go unpunished.

The blood of the prophets

The Triune God had judged Ahab and Jezebel for their promotion of a false religion and for persecuting His people. But this did not deter other kings – both in Israel and Judah

10   Psalm 2: 12

11   See also 1 Kings 21 & 22, 2 Kings 9: 30-37, and 2 Kings 10: 1-17.

– from using the power of the state to advance the worship of idols and seeking to quash those who trusted in the LORD Jesus.

For example, in Judah, Zechariah the priest was martyred by King Joash for seeking to call Judah back to the LORD Jesus. Joash had served the LORD faithfully for much of his reign, during the years of Jehoiada the priest – who was Zechariah's father. The king restored the temple from Baal so that it served its true purpose of witnessing to the suffering of the Messiah. 'As long as Jehoiada lived, burnt offerings were presented continually in the temple of the LORD' (2 Chronicles 24: 14). But then:

> After the death of Jehoiada, the officials of Judah came and paid homage to the king, and he listened to them. They abandoned the temple of the Lord, the God of their ancestors, and worshipped Asherah poles and idols. Because of their guilt, God's anger came on Judah and Jerusalem. Although the Lord sent prophets to the people to bring them back to him, and though they testified against them, they would not listen.

> Then the Spirit of God came on Zechariah son of Jehoiada the priest. He stood before the people and said, 'This is what God says: "Why do you disobey the LORD's commands? You will not prosper. Because you have forsaken the LORD, he has forsaken you."'

> But they plotted against him, and by order of the king they stoned him to death in the courtyard of the LORD's temple. King Joash did not remember the kindness Zechariah's father Jehoiada had shown him but killed his son, who said as he lay dying, 'May the LORD see this and call you to account'. (2 Chronicles 24: 17-22)

Zechariah's last words demonstrated his faith that His LORD and Saviour would avenge the shedding of his blood; that there would be justice.

Isaiah was ignored and rejected despite the wonderful prophecies he gave of the LORD Jesus' glory and suffering:[12]

> He was despised and rejected by mankind,
>> a man of suffering, and familiar with pain.
> Like one from whom people hide their faces
>> he was despised, and we held him in low esteem.
>
> Surely he took up our pain
>> and bore our suffering,
> yet we considered him punished by God,
>> stricken by him, and afflicted.
> But he was pierced for our transgressions,
>> he was crushed for our iniquities;
> the punishment that brought us peace was on him,
>> and by his wounds we are healed.
> We all, like sheep, have gone astray,
>> each of us has turned to our own way;
> and the Lord has laid on him
>> the iniquity of us all.
>
> He was oppressed and afflicted,
>> yet he did not open his mouth;
> he was led like a lamb to the slaughter,
>> and as a sheep before its shearers is silent,
>> so he did not open his mouth.
> By oppression and judgment he was taken away.
>> Yet who of his generation protested?
> For he was cut off from the land of the living;

---

12   See Isaiah 6 and John 12: 37-41.

for the transgression of my people he was punished.
He was assigned a grave with the wicked,
    and with the rich in his death,
though he had done no violence,
    nor was any deceit in his mouth.

Yet it was the Lord's will to crush him and cause him to suffer,
    and though the Lord makes his life an offering for sin,
he will see his offspring and prolong his days,
    and the will of the Lord will prosper in his hand.
After he has suffered,
    he will see the light of life and be satisfied;
by his knowledge my righteous servant will justify many,
    and he will bear their iniquities.
Therefore I will give him a portion among the great,
    and he will divide the spoils with the strong,
because he poured out his life unto death,
    and was numbered with the transgressors.
For he bore the sin of many,
    and made intercession for the transgressors.
(Isaiah 53: 3-12)

Jeremiah, another faithful prophet who foretold the coming of the Righteous Branch[13], and who repeatedly warned Judah of its fate if it did not turn back to the LORD, suffered persecution of various kinds at the hands of the religious authorities. He made clear that if the people did not repent they would be taken into exile and Jerusalem would be destroyed. Yet:

When the priest Pashhur son of Immer, the official in charge of the temple of the LORD, heard Jeremiah prophesying these things, he had Jeremiah the prophet

---

13   Jeremiah 23: 1-6.

beaten and put in the stocks at the Upper Gate of Benjamin at the LORD's temple (Jeremiah 20: 1-2)[14].

And on another occasion when the LORD warned the people through Jeremiah of the curse that was to fall on the land:

The priests, the prophets and all the people seized [Jeremiah] and said, 'You must die! Why do you prophesy in the LORD's name that this house will be like Shiloh and this city will be desolate and deserted?' And all the people crowded around Jeremiah in the house of the LORD. (Jeremiah 26: 8-9)

The LORD provided Jeremiah with some protection against these attacks: but other prophets suffered the fate of Zechariah.[15] Every prophet faced danger. The LORD was determined to give His people every opportunity to repent and turn to Him, but His prophets faced hard hearts and deaf ears:

The LORD, the God of their ancestors, sent word to them through his messengers again and again, because he had pity on his people and on his dwelling-place. But they mocked God's messengers, despised his words and scoffed at his prophets until the wrath of the LORD was aroused against his people and there was no remedy. (2 Chronicles 36: 15-16)

Ignoring the Triune God's gracious call to life, the people were taken off into captivity[16].

---

14 Jeremiah 20:7-18 sets out the prophet's complaint to the LORD about his suffering and his testimony that the LORD 'rescues the life of the needy from the hands of the wicked'.

15 See Jeremiah 26: 20-23 and the whole chapter. We read of other attacks on Jeremiah in 18: 18-23, and chapters 37-38.

16 2 Kings 24-25, 2 Chronicles 36

Living Blood

A separate chapter could be written on each of the prophets named above. The Holy Spirit is certainly keen to remind the Church in every generation of their suffering for Christ:

> [The people] were disobedient and rebelled against you; they turned their backs on your law. They killed your prophets, who had warned them in order to turn them back to you; they committed awful blasphemies (Nehemiah 9: 26).

> 'You stiff-necked people! Your hearts and ears are still uncircumcised. You are just like your ancestors: you always resist the Holy Spirit! Was there ever a prophet your ancestors did not persecute? They even killed those who predicted the coming of the Righteous One' (Acts 7: 51-52).

The Spirit does not want us to forget the example of faith in the LORD Jesus that the prophets showed in the face of their suffering. 'Brothers and sisters, as an example of patience in the face of suffering, take the prophets who spoke in the name of the Lord' (James 5: 10).

> And what more shall I say? I do not have time to tell about Gideon, Barak, Samson and Jephthah, about David and Samuel and the prophets, who through faith conquered kingdoms, administered justice, and gained what was promised; who shut the mouths of lions, quenched the fury of the flames, and escaped the edge of the sword; whose weakness was turned to strength; and who became powerful in battle and routed foreign armies. Women received back their dead, raised to life again. There were others who were tortured, refusing to be released so that they might gain an even better

resurrection. Some faced jeers and flogging, and even chains and imprisonment. They were put to death by stoning; they were sawn in two; they were killed by the sword. They went about in sheepskins and goatskins, destitute, persecuted and ill-treated – the world was not worthy of them. They wandered in deserts and mountains, living in caves and in holes in the ground.

These were all commended for their faith, yet none of them received what had been promised, since God had planned something better for us so that only together with us would they be made perfect.

Therefore, since we are surrounded by such a great cloud of witnesses, let us throw off everything that hinders and the sin that so easily entangles. And let us run with perseverance the race marked out for us, fixing our eyes on Jesus, the pioneer and perfecter of faith. For the joy that was set before him he endured the cross, scorning its shame, and sat down at the right hand of the throne of God. Consider him who endured such opposition from sinners, so that you will not grow weary and lose heart (Hebrews 11: 32-40, 12: 1-3).

The Triune God does not forget the persecution of His people. When the Word of God – the Angel of the LORD – was sent into the world as a human being, He warned that those who persecuted Him have a common identity with the persecutors from previous generations. And they would all be judged for their treatment of His people:

'Woe to you, teachers of the law and Pharisees, you hypocrites! You build tombs for the prophets and decorate the graves of the righteous. And you say, "If we had lived in the days of our ancestors, we would not have taken part with them in shedding the blood of the prophets." So you testify against yourselves that you are the descendants of those who murdered the prophets. Go ahead, then, and complete what your ancestors started!

'You snakes! You brood of vipers! How will you escape being condemned to hell? Therefore I am sending you prophets and sages and teachers. Some of them you will kill and crucify; others you will flog in your synagogues and pursue from town to town. And so upon you will come all the righteous blood that has been shed on earth, from the blood of righteous Abel to the blood of Zechariah son of Berekiah, whom you murdered between the temple and the altar. Truly I tell you, all this will come upon this generation'. (Matthew 23: 29-36)

From the very beginning the devil hated the righteous blood of Christ the Seed, which gave life to His people. And so Satan has enticed his followers to shed the blood of Christ's followers. But there will be a reckoning for that blood, just as the LORD God demanded justice from those who persecuted Elijah, Zechariah, and the other prophets of Israel and Judah. Ahab was destroyed. Jezebel was destroyed. And so on the great Day of Judgement, all those who have drunk 'the blood of God's holy people, the blood of those who bore testimony to Jesus' will be given 'blood to drink as they deserve' (Rev 16: 5-6, 17: 5-6).

Evil will be evicted from the world. The LORD and His Church will prevail.

CHAPTER EIGHT

WHEN THE KING IS THE RELIGION

Polycarp, the 2nd-century Christian bishop of Smyrna, was martyred for refusing to burn incense to the Roman Emperor because of his faith in Christ. Shortly before his death, the proconsul urged Polycarp to pledge allegiance to Caesar, saying, "Swear, and I will set thee at liberty, reproach Christ;" Polycarp declared, "Eighty and six years have I served Him, and He never did me any injury: how then can I blaspheme my King and my Saviour?" The proconsul told Polycarp he would set wild beasts on him if he did not repent and when he didn't, the threat changed to fire. But Polycarp said,

> "Thou threatenest me with fire which burneth for an hour, and after a little is extinguished, but thou art ignorant of the fire of the coming judgment and of eternal punishment, reserved for the ungodly. But why tarriest thou? Bring forth what thou wilt."

As Polycarp faced the fire, he prayed as follows: "O Lord God Almighty, the Father of thy beloved and blessed Son Jesus Christ, by whom we have received the knowledge of Thee... I give Thee thanks that Thou hast counted me, worthy of this day and this hour, that I should have a part in the number of Thy martyrs, in the cup of thy Christ, to the resurrection of eternal life, both of soul and body... Wherefore also I praise Thee for all things, I bless Thee, I glorify Thee, along with the everlasting and heavenly Jesus Christ, Thy beloved Son, with whom, to Thee, and the Holy Ghost, be glory both now and to all coming ages. Amen."

Polycarp was bound and burned at the stake, then stabbed when the fire failed to touch him[1].

Polycarp's is an old story; but one can find similar such stories happening right now in the world – in those countries ruled by someone who believes that they are divine. There is no room for Christians in a land when the king thinks he is God. And that is what we learn from the book of Daniel, which highlights the dangers for believers in the LORD Jesus when the king commands that he should be worshipped. Yet the Scriptures also reveal God the Father, Son and Spirit's loving protection of His people.

The Church in Exile

The prophets had implored Israel and Judah to stay faithful to the LORD Jesus. But neither kingdom listened to the warnings given to them; and first Israel, and then Judah were sent by the LORD into exile:

1   The Martyrdom of Polycarp, 150-160 A.D, Roberts-Donaldson English Translation, [Online] Available: athttp://www.earlychristianwritings.com/text/martyrdompolycarp-roberts.html [2019, January]

He brought up against them the king of the Babylonians, who killed their young men with the sword in the sanctuary, and did not spare young men or young women, the elderly or the infirm. God gave them all into the hands of Nebuchadnezzar. He carried to Babylon all the articles from the temple of God, both large and small, and the treasures of the LORD's temple and the treasures of the king and his officials. They set fire to God's temple and broke down the wall of Jerusalem; they burned all the palaces and destroyed everything of value there.

He carried into exile to Babylon the remnant, who escaped from the sword, and they became servants to him and his successors until the kingdom of Persia came to power. The land enjoyed its sabbath rests; all the time of its desolation it rested, until the seventy years were completed in fulfilment of the word of the LORD spoken by Jeremiah' (2 Chronicles 36: 17-21).

To those involved in these events at the time, they must have seemed like an exercise of power by the Babylonians. Yet the Triune God was sovereign over the king of Babylon. He had promised that the people would go into exile and He promised – through the word spoken by Jeremiah[2] – that they would return in exactly 70 years. In the meantime, the responsibility of His people was to live in the foreign land as the LORD had instructed them (again through the prophet Jeremiah):

This is the text of the letter that the prophet Jeremiah sent from Jerusalem to the surviving elders among the exiles and to the priests, the prophets and all the other people Nebuchadnezzar had carried into exile from

2   Jeremiah 25: 1-12 and 29: 10-14.

Jerusalem to Babylon. (This was after King Jehoiachin and the queen mother, the court officials and the leaders of Judah and Jerusalem, the skilled workers and the craftsmen had gone into exile from Jerusalem.) He entrusted the letter to Elasah son of Shaphan and to Gemariah son of Hilkiah, whom Zedekiah king of Judah sent to King Nebuchadnezzar in Babylon. It said:

This is what the LORD Almighty, the God of Israel, says to all those I carried into exile from Jerusalem to Babylon: 'Build houses and settle down; plant gardens and eat what they produce. Marry and have sons and daughters; find wives for your sons and give your daughters in marriage, so that they too may have sons and daughters. Increase in number there; do not decrease. Also, seek the peace and prosperity of the city to which I have carried you into exile. Pray to the LORD for it, because if it prospers, you too will prosper.' (Jeremiah 29: 1-7.)

The Church was called to live quietly for the LORD, seeking His blessing upon the land in which they lived. They were not to start a revolution; to seek to overthrow the government in order that they might impose their cultural agenda on other people. They were to live for the LORD Jesus, being His ambassadors; serving the rulers He had appointed, serving the neighbours He had given them, and witnessing to Him.

Yet living for the LORD Jesus was likely to put the people's lives in danger if the country in which they lived did not tolerate the worship of Christ – if it was obligatory to worship another god. It would be especially dangerous if the king of that land regarded himself as god and demanded that the people bowed down to him. And it was exactly that situation that the followers of the LORD had to face in Babylon.

Nebuchadnezzar's Dream

Nebuchadnezzar was the name of the Babylonian king who had taken the Israelites into his kingdom. He was keen to find a use for these human assets, and he brought a number of them into his service. The Scriptures tell us that, among those chosen, Shadrach, Meshach, Abednego, and Daniel were found by the king to be full of wisdom and understanding.[3]

One night the king had a dream and he promised to give rewards and honour to anyone who could give its meaning[4]. The dream was of a large statute, with a head of gold, its chest and arms of silver, its belly and thighs of silver; its legs of iron; its feet partly of iron and partly of baked clay. The statue was awesome in appearance yet was smashed to pieces by a rock, uncut by human hands, which became a huge mountain and filled the whole earth.

In interpreting the dream, Daniel told Nebuchadnezzar that *he* was the head of gold:

> You are the king of kings. The God of heaven has given you dominion and power and might and glory; in your hands he has placed all mankind and the beasts of the field and the birds in the sky. Wherever they live, he has made you ruler over them all. (Daniel 2: 37-38)

Yet Nebuchadnezzar's kingdom would not last forever, Daniel said. Other kingdoms would come and go until the Uncreated Rock would appear and destroy all the kingdoms of sinful humanity.

> The God of heaven will set up a kingdom that will never be destroyed, nor will it be left to another people. It will crush all these other kingdoms and bring them to an end but it will itself endure for ever. (Daniel 2: 44)

---

3   Daniel 1: 17-20

4   Daniel 2: 1-6.

This eternal kingdom was the one which the Messiah would secure – by taking the same flesh as humanity and dying and rising again. God the Father had made a promise to David about the Messiah: 'I will establish his kingdom... and I will establish the throne of his kingdom for ever. I will be his Father, and He shall be my Son' (2 Samuel 7: 12-14). Now God confirmed the promise in the dream given to Daniel.

What a message of comfort for Daniel and his fellow Israelites as they resided in exile. The eternal kingdom of the Messiah was more powerful than Babylon, however mighty it might appear. They were part of His kingdom wherever they lived. The LORD was their King. He was ruling over Babylon; He was ruling the whole universe. Their trust was in the Divine King.

The Church had nothing to fear from Nebuchadnezzar. Those not following the LORD Jesus might fear him and his power but, as the LORD had spoken through Isaiah, 'Do not fear what they fear, and do not dread it. The LORD Almighty is the one you are to regard as holy, He is the one you are to fear, He is the one you are to dread'[5]. The Church was called to revere Christ as Lord. All who trusted in Christ the Rock would never be put to shame; yet the very same Rock caused those who did not believe to stumble[6].

Worshipping Nebuchadnezzar

Superficially, Nebuchadnezzar seemed to acknowledge the greatness of the LORD. He said to Daniel, 'Surely your God is the God of gods and the Lord of kings and a revealer of mysteries, for you were able to reveal this mystery

---

5   Isaiah 8: 12-13. These words of Isaiah called the Church to do good even if they suffered for it. See 1 Peter 3: 13-15.

6   Isaiah 28:16, Isaiah 8:14.

(Daniel 2: 47). The king made Daniel 'ruler over the entire province of Babylon and placed him in charge of all its wise men' and 'at Daniel's request the king appointed Shadrach, Meshach and Abednego chief ministers over the province of Babylon, while Daniel himself remained at the royal court' (Daniel 2: 48-49).

But this was just political shrewdness on Nebuchadnezzar's part. In his heart the king believed that *he* was the King of kings and God of gods. The lesson of Nebuchadnezzar's dream had been that the Kingdom of the Rock would destroy the kingdoms represented by the statue with the golden head and feet of iron and clay. Yet Nebuchadnezzar's response was to build an all-gold statue! It was as though he wanted to convince people that he was more powerful than the Rock; that his kingdom could last forever; that he was God.

> King Nebuchadnezzar made an image of gold, sixty cubits high and six cubits wide, and set it up on the plain of Dura in the province of Babylon. He then summoned the satraps, prefects, governors, advisors, treasurers, judges, magistrates and all the other provincial officials to come to the dedication of the image he had set up. So the satraps, prefects, governors, advisors, treasurers, judges, magistrates and all the other provincial officials assembled for the dedication of the image that King Nebuchadnezzar had set up, and they stood before it.
>
> Then the herald loudly proclaimed, 'Nations and peoples of every language, this is what you are commanded to do: as soon as you hear the sound of the horn, flute, zither, lyre, harp, pipe and all kinds of music, you must

fall down and worship the image of gold that King Nebuchadnezzar has set up. Whoever does not fall down and worship will immediately be thrown into a blazing furnace.' (Daniel 3: 1-6)

We are not told the identity of the golden image but it seems likely that it was of King Nebuchadnezzar himself; certainly the purpose of the image was that the people had to worship it at the king's command. Bow down or die, was the command. The king demanded that all his people gave their devotion to him. And most, whether enthusiastically or reluctantly, obeyed the king's command:

Therefore, as soon as they heard the sound of the horn, flute, zither, lyre, harp and all kinds of music, all the nations and peoples of every language fell down and worshipped the image of gold that King Nebuchadnezzar had set up. (Daniel 3: 7)

Yet not everyone was obedient, as the king was told:

At this time some astrologers came forward and denounced the Jews. They said to King Nebuchadnezzar, 'May the king live for ever! Your Majesty has issued a decree that everyone who hears the sound of the horn, flute, zither, lyre, harp, pipe and all kinds of music must fall down and worship the image of gold, and that whoever does not fall down and worship will be thrown into a blazing furnace. But there are some Jews whom you have set over the affairs of the province of Babylon – Shadrach, Meshach and Abednego – who pay no attention to you, Your Majesty. They neither serve your gods nor worship the image of gold you have set up.' (Daniel 3: 9-12)

Facing the Fire

No doubt other Israelites, including Daniel, also refused to bow the knee to Nebuchadnezzar's statue, but punishment fell on Shadrach, Meshach and Abednego:

> Furious with rage, Nebuchadnezzar summoned Shadrach, Meshach and Abednego. So these men were brought before the king, and Nebuchadnezzar said to them, 'Is it true, Shadrach, Meshach and Abednego, that you do not serve my gods or worship the image of gold I have set up? Now when you hear the sound of the horn, flute, zither, lyre, harp, pipe and all kinds of music, if you are ready to fall down and worship the image I made, very good. But if you do not worship it, you will be thrown immediately into a blazing furnace. Then what god will be able to rescue you from my hand?' (Daniel 3: 13-15)

The three men were confronted with the awful dilemma that so many followers of the LORD Jesus face: *Renounce Christ or die!* But they remembered the message of Nebuchadnezzar's dream. They knew that God's eternal kingdom would outlast and defeat all the kingdoms of the world, and all the sinful kings who run them. How could they possibly renounce their faith?! To do so would be to forsake the true King of the universe. To do so would be to renounce true life – the eternal life given by the Messiah, the One who was to save them from a fire far worse than Nebuchadnezzar's: the fire which destroys souls as well as bodies.[7]

Whatever the temptation they must have faced to avoid this barbaric persecution, the three men trusted in their LORD:

---

7   'Do not be afraid of those who kill the body but cannot kill the soul. Rather, be afraid of the One who can destroy both soul and body in hell.' (Matthew 10: 28).

> Shadrach, Meshach and Abednego replied to him, 'King Nebuchadnezzar, we do not need to defend ourselves before you in this matter. If we are thrown into the blazing furnace, the God we serve is able to deliver us from it, and he will deliver us from Your Majesty's hand. But even if he does not, we want you to know, Your Majesty, that we will not serve your gods or worship the image of gold you have set up.' (Daniel 3: 16-18.)

The three men knew the LORD God *could* save them from persecution; but they did not presume that the LORD would do so. It was not for them to say what He must or must not do. They knew that it was not His will to keep every believer from persecution. The followers of the Messiah must be prepared to follow the way of suffering, the way of the altar.

Shadrach, Meshach and Abednego were confident that the LORD their God would do whatever He thought best. He was their Saviour. Trusting in the LORD Jesus, they would not bow the knee to Babylon's king. Their lack of fear of his ability to kill them radically undermined his power, much to his anger.

> Then Nebuchadnezzar was furious with Shadrach, Meshach and Abednego, and his attitude towards them changed. He ordered the furnace to be heated seven times hotter than usual and commanded some of the strongest soldiers in his army to tie up Shadrach, Meshach and Abednego and throw them into the blazing furnace. So these men, wearing their robes, trousers, turbans and other clothes, were bound and thrown into the blazing furnace. The king's command was so urgent and the furnace so hot that the flames of the fire killed the soldiers who took up Shadrach, Meshach and Abednego, and these three men, firmly tied, fell into the blazing furnace. (Daniel 3: 19-23)

There was still time for the three Israelites to 'repent' and turn to Nebuchadnezzar. A few words would have done it. 'Stop!', 'Wait!', 'We will obey you!'. They were walking towards an awful, excoriatingly painful death. Yet they remained silent; faithful to their LORD. What Psalm would they have sung as they were about to enter the furnace? Perhaps they echoed Christ's prophetic words from Psalm 18, as He looked forward to His salvation from death:

> The Lord is my rock, my fortress and my deliverer;
>> my God is my rock, in whom I take refuge,
>> my shield and the horn of my salvation, my
> stronghold.
>
> I called to the Lord, who is worthy of praise,
>> and I have been saved from my enemies.
> The cords of death entangled me;
>> the torrents of destruction overwhelmed me...
> In my distress I called to the Lord;
>> I cried to my God for help.
> From his temple he heard my voice;
>> my cry came before him, into his ears...
> He parted the heavens and came down...
> (Psalm 18: 1-2, 6, 9)

Fellowship in the Furnace

The men entered the furnace. But the LORD of heaven did not allow them to enter alone, as the king himself suddenly spotted:

> Then King Nebuchadnezzar leaped to his feet in amazement and asked his advisors, 'Weren't there three men that we tied up and threw into the fire?'

They replied, 'Certainly, Your Majesty.'

He said, 'Look! I see four men walking around in the fire, unbound and unharmed, and the fourth looks like a son of the gods.'

Nebuchadnezzar then approached the opening of the blazing furnace and shouted, 'Shadrach, Meshach and Abednego, servants of the Most High God, come out! Come here!'

So Shadrach, Meshach and Abednego came out of the fire, and the satraps, prefects, governors and royal advisors crowded around them. They saw that the fire had not harmed their bodies, nor was a hair of their heads singed; their robes were not scorched, and there was no smell of fire on them.

Then Nebuchadnezzar said, 'Praise be to the God of Shadrach, Meshach and Abednego, who has sent his angel and rescued his servants! They trusted in him and defied the king's command and were willing to give up their lives rather than serve or worship any god except their own God'. (Daniel 3: 24-28)

The LORD of heaven had looked down and seen that His servants were suffering and He sent His Angel to stand with them in the fire. The LORD sent the God-man; the Son of God[8]. He wanted to demonstrate His love for His children; to show His unity with them; that to persecute them was to persecute Him. 'In all their distress He too was distressed, and the Angel of His Presence saved them'[9].

---

8   The King James Version translates Daniel 3: 25 as 'Son of God' rather than 'son of gods' as used by the NIV.

9   Isaiah 63: 9.

What a night of fellowship Shadrach, Meshach and Abednego must have enjoyed with the LORD Jesus. As long as Christ remained with them, they didn't want to leave the fire. The king had to order them to come out from the furnace!

He found them completely unharmed[10]. The Angel had ensured that the fire did not make not a single mark on them.

Seeing the saving work of the Angel in the fire revealed the true identity of God to Nebuchadnezzar. God was not aloof and impersonal, a statue of gold or bronze; the LORD Jesus was sent by the LORD in heaven to stand in the fire to save His people. He was the Mediator between God and humanity. The Spirit opened Nebuchadnezzar's heart and he gave praise to 'the God of Shadrach, Meshach and Abednego', marvelling that the men 'trusted in Him and defied the king's command and were willing to give up their lives rather than serve or worship any god except their own God' (Daniel 3: 28).

The king was overwhelmed by the faith of Shadrach, Meshach and Abednego which had led them to disobey him. Their courage forced him to do business with the LORD their God. What an extraordinary God whose servants do such extraordinary things.

Standing firm for Christ had brought the three Israelites into conflict with Nebuchadnezzar when he believed he was god. Now, as he turned to the LORD, he commended their faith and praised *their* God. Such was his enthusiasm for the LORD, the king outlawed any criticism of Him:

10   'Everyone will hate you because of me. But not a hair of your head will
     perish. Stand firm, and you will win life.' (Luke 21:17-19)

> 'Therefore I decree that the people of any nation or
> language who say anything against the God of Shadrach,
> Meshach and Abednego be cut into pieces and their
> houses be turned into piles of rubble, for no other god
> can save in this way.' Then the king promoted Shadrach,
> Meshach and Abednego in the province of Babylon.
> (Daniel 3: 29-30)

Having used the power of the state to prevent the Jews
from believing in the true and living God, the king now
wanted to make it illegal not to believe in Him!
Nebuchadnezzar hadn't yet grasped that true faith came
through the power of the Spirit not political power.
He seemed to think that no-one would believe unless he
commanded it; that *he* was the key to true belief among the
people. This new servant of the LORD needed to cut out
from his heart his obsession with his power – something
which later the LORD graciously helped him to do[11]. And so
Nebuchadnezzar turned from being a persecutor of the true
and living God and His servants to someone who testified to
His grace. He said:

> Now I, Nebuchadnezzar, praise and exalt and glorify the
> King of heaven, because everything he does is right and
> all his ways are just. And those who walk in pride he is
> able to humble.(Daniel 4: 37)

Daniel faces the Lions

As Daniel had prophesied when interpreting
Nebuchadnezzar's dream, Babylon waned in its importance.
It was taken into the Persian empire under Cyrus, and
Nebuchadnezzar's dynasty ended. Darius, a Mede by

---

11   See Daniel 4

background, took over the kingdom of Babylon.[12] Despite these changes, Daniel retained his position of authority and respect:

> It pleased Darius to appoint 120 satraps to rule throughout the kingdom, with three chief ministers over them, one of whom was Daniel. The satraps were made accountable to them so that the king might not suffer loss. Now Daniel so distinguished himself among the chief ministers and the satraps by his exceptional qualities that the king planned to set him over the whole kingdom. At this, the chief ministers and the satraps tried to find grounds for charges against Daniel in his conduct of government affairs, but they were unable to do so. They could find no corruption in him, because he was trustworthy and neither corrupt nor negligent. Finally these men said, 'We will never find any basis for charges against this man Daniel unless it has something to do with the law of his God.' (Daniel 6: 1-5)

Daniel continued to serve the kingdom to be best of his ability. He was obedient to the LORD's command to seek 'the peace and prosperity' of the land in which he lived in exile (Jeremiah 29: 7). It was the LORD he served; he did not work to gain the good opinion of those around him. Yet it was that very attitude of selfless service of the LORD which made Daniel such a valuable and trusted worker. He so impressed Darius that the king was prepared to put this Israelite in sole charge of the kingdom. Yet his fellow civil servants hated him; partly no doubt out of jealousy; but also motivated by the irrational anger that those who do not love Christ direct towards His followers. The civil servants

---

12   Daniel 5: 30-31

continued the on-going war of Satan against Christ and His followers. And their hatred of Daniel and his God led to a plan of murder:

> So these chief ministers and satraps went as a group to the king and said: 'May King Darius live for ever! The royal ministers, prefects, satraps, advisors and governors have all agreed that the king should issue an edict and enforce the decree that anyone who prays to any god or human being during the next thirty days, except to you, Your Majesty, shall be thrown into the lions' den. Now, Your Majesty, issue the decree and put it in writing so that it cannot be altered – in accordance with the law of the Medes and Persians, which cannot be repealed.' So King Darius put the decree in writing. (Daniel 6: 6-9).

Darius did not need much persuasion to put into law a command which made it compulsory to worship him! It had an obvious attraction. The law was simple. All who did not worship the king were to be destroyed. The king was God. He was to be revered and obeyed.

Once more the followers of Christ faced persecution – there was no space allowed for them to worship the LORD. If they did so, they faced certain death in the lions' den, as Shadrach, Meshach and Abednego had faced death in the blazing furnace for not bowing down to Nebuchadnezzar's statue. But it did not deter Daniel:

> Now when Daniel learned that the decree had been published, he went home to his upstairs room where the windows opened towards Jerusalem. Three times a day he got down on his knees and prayed, giving thanks to his God, just as he had done before. (Daniel 6: 6-9)

It was Daniel's daily habit to pray to the true and living God. Three times a day he looked towards Jerusalem, not for superstitious reasons, but because it focused his thoughts on the Messiah, whose work of salvation opened up access to the Most Holy Place. Because of the work of the Messiah, Daniel could ascend to heaven and talk to God Most High. And thrice daily, he gave thanks to His Father through the Messiah for His salvation and grace.

There were several choices that faced Daniel in the light of Darius's decree. He could have resigned his position; organised an insurrection; bowed his knee to the king; or he could have made sure he did his prayers in secret.

But he chose to carry on living exactly as he had done before the edict. He had only ever obeyed the king because of his faith in the LORD Jesus; now his faith drove him to disobey Darius. But he made no public demonstration of his rebellion; he did not want to draw attention to himself or coerce others to follow his way. He just wanted to keep his eyes fixed on his LORD.

Faith in the Eternal Kingdom

How did Daniel have the courage to endure this persecution?

In His grace, the LORD had prepared his servant to face this moment of trial. He had given him – and, through him, the Church in every age – a number of visions which repeated and expanded the themes of Nebuchadnezzar's dream.

The visions (recorded in Daniel 7 to 12) demonstrated the LORD's complete sovereignty over the kingdoms of the world. These kingdoms would rise and fall in importance; they would inflict suffering on followers of the LORD yet they would be ultimately defeated by the eternal kingdom of the Messiah. Daniel was shown that God the Father – the Ancient of Days – reigned in heaven, full of awesome glory and holiness. No ordinary man could survive in His presence but, Daniel said:

> In my vision at night I looked, and there before me was one like a Son of Man, coming with the clouds of heaven. He approached the Ancient of Days and was led into his presence. He was given authority, glory and sovereign power; all nations and peoples of every language worshipped him. His dominion is an everlasting dominion that will not pass away, and his kingdom is one that will never be destroyed. (Daniel 7: 13-14).

The Son of Man could approach the Ancient of Days. This Man could act as Mediator between the Ancient of Days and humanity. He – the Anointed One – would 'put an end to sin... atone for wickedness... bring in everlasting righteousness... [He would] be put to death and... have nothing... until the end that is decreed is poured out on him'[13]. To the victorious Son of Man would be given an everlasting dominion – comprising people of all nations – which would never pass away.

In his vision, Daniel saw *the* Man – Christ Himself – 'a man dressed in linen, with a belt of fine gold from Uphaz round his waist. His body was like topaz, his face like lightning, his eyes like flaming torches, his arms and legs like the gleam of burnished bronze, and his voice like the sound of a multitude' (Daniel 10: 5-6). Who could not be encouraged by that sight as they faced the totalitarian power of Darius? Christ could never be defeated.

---

13   Daniel 9: 20-27

Daniel also saw in his dream a representative of all the political rulers of the world who would suppress God's people. This king would:

> speak against the Most High and oppress his holy people and try to change the set times and the laws. The holy people will be delivered into his hands for a time, times and half a time (Daniel 7: 25).

The saints would face suffering for a 'time, times and half a time' i.e. for a time which would feel long enough but was strictly limited by the Triune God. He would not allow their persecution to last for long; compared to life in the 'eternal dominion' it would be a very short time. The king who persecuted God's people would be dealt with by the Son of Man soon enough:

> The court will sit, and his power will be taken away and completely destroyed for ever. Then the sovereignty, power and greatness of all the kingdoms under heaven will be handed over to the holy people of the Most High. His kingdom will be an everlasting kingdom, and all rulers will worship and obey him (Daniel 7: 26-27)[14].

The saints would no longer be subject to a tyrannical king; his paper kingdom would be blown away and the Church would enjoy the freedom of the eternal Kingdom purchased by the Anointed One; each one having their own inheritance in this glorious new creation.[15]

The Lions' Den

The Spirit of the LORD gave Daniel these visions to sustain the Church through its times of persecution. Whatever

---

14   See also Daniel 8: 15-24

15   Daniel 12: 13

suffering it faced, the Church knew that it would not be defeated. The Ancient of Days remained on His throne; the Son of Man sat with Him, enabling the saints to sit in the presence of the Most High. No attack of a human king could separate the Church from its King.

Thus Daniel, when faced with the edict to stop worshipping the true God or face death, carried on praying to Him. This was exactly the time when he needed to depend on the LORD. He needed to pray for His help, and he could do so with confidence that the Son of Man would intercede for him before the Ancient of Days.

But those who were determined to persecute Daniel were delighted to see him praying. As far as they were concerned, he had fallen into their trap:

> They went to the king and spoke to him about his royal decree: 'Did you not publish a decree that during the next thirty days anyone who prays to any god or human being except to you, Your Majesty, would be thrown into the lions' den?'
>
> The king answered, 'The decree stands – in accordance with the law of the Medes and Persians, which cannot be repealed.'
>
> Then they said to the king, 'Daniel, who is one of the exiles from Judah, pays no attention to you, Your Majesty, or to the decree you put in writing. He still prays three times a day.' When the king heard this, he was greatly distressed; he was determined to rescue Daniel and made every effort until sunset to save him.
>
> Then the men went as a group to King Darius and said to him, 'Remember, Your Majesty, that according to the law of the Medes and Persians no decree or edict that the king issues can be changed.' So the king gave the order,

> and they brought Daniel and threw him into the lions'
> den. The king said to Daniel, 'May your God, whom you
> serve continually, rescue you!'. (Daniel 6: 12-16)

How weak and foolish the powerful are. Darius had been
persuaded by his officials that he should be regarded as a
deity – someone whom the whole land should worship. Now
Darius admitted there was nothing he could do to save
Daniel; he was powerless!

The only source of hope in this mess was the God of
Daniel – the One to whom, Darius had ordained, people
were not to pray. It seems possible that king broke his own
law and himself prayed to God Most High for Daniel:

> A stone was brought and placed over the mouth of the
> den, and the king sealed it with his own signet ring and
> with the rings of his nobles, so that Daniel's situation
> might not be changed. Then the king returned to his
> palace and spent the night without eating and without
> any entertainment being brought to him. And he could
> not sleep.

> At the first light of dawn, the king got up and hurried to
> the lions' den. When he came near the den, he called to
> Daniel in an anguished voice, 'Daniel, servant of the
> living God, has your God, whom you serve continually,
> been able to rescue you from the lions?'

> Daniel answered, 'May the king live for ever![16] My God
> sent his Angel, and he shut the mouths of the lions. They
> have not hurt me, because I was found innocent in his
> sight. Nor have I ever done any wrong before you, Your
> Majesty.'

---

16   Darius' officials used those words when addressing Darius to signal that
     the king was a god. One imagines that Daniel used the phrase to call
     Darius to trust in the Messiah and enjoy the eternal life that His
     resurrection from death earnt for His followers.

> The king was overjoyed and gave orders to lift Daniel out
> of the den. And when Daniel was lifted from the den, no
> wound was found on him, because he had trusted in his
> God. (Daniel 6: 17-23)

Daniel's body was put in the den and a stone rolled across it.
He was as good as dead. But he returned from the tomb
alive! As Shadrach, Meshach and Abednego had escaped
from the burning furnace without a mark on them, so Daniel
came out from the lion's den without a single scratch.
'Figuratively speaking' he had been resurrected[17].

Daniel's salvation was a prophecy of the saving work of
the Messiah – the One who would suffer despite His
innocence, and yet, trusting in His Father, who would walk
through the shadow of death. He was sent by God Most
High to save His people, as He was sent by God to save
Daniel from death.

Daniel, like Shadrach, Meshach and Abednego before
him, had the privilege of enjoying a night of fellowship with
the LORD Jesus – in contrast to Darius who had suffered a
night of torment. Better to be in a lion's den with Christ than
a palace without Him.

Daniel had been saved by the LORD. Afterwards justice
was administered to his persecutors – to those who had
sought to murder the followers of the LORD; those who
hated the LORD Himself. Yet again the Triune God showed
that He would not allow those who persecuted His followers
to get away with their evil:

> At the king's command, the men who had falsely
> accused Daniel were brought in and thrown into the
> lions' den, along with their wives and children. And

---

17   Hebrews 11: 19. See also 11: 32-35.

before they reached the floor of the den, the lions overpowered them and crushed all their bones.
(Daniel 6: 24)

Darius is saved

But what about Darius? In His mercy, God Most High dealt with his evil by turning him to be a follower of the LORD Jesus. The king had witnessed the faith and grace of Daniel; he had seen Daniel being saved by the Angel of the LORD from death; and so he put his trust in the LORD. Like Nebuchadnezzar, Darius was overwhelmed by what he saw the LORD doing through His people. By the power of the Spirit he changed from being a persecutor of God's people to a witness to His grace, proclaiming His greatness to all the nations of the world:

> Then King Darius wrote to all the nations and peoples of every language in all the earth:
>
> 'May you prosper greatly!
>
> I issue a decree that in every part of my kingdom people must fear and reverence the God of Daniel.
>
> For he is the living God
> and he endures for ever;
> his kingdom will not be destroyed,
> his dominion will never end.
> He rescues and he saves;
> he performs signs and wonders
> in the heavens and on the earth.
> He has rescued Daniel
> from the power of the lions.'
>
> So Daniel prospered during the reign of Darius and the reign of Cyrus the Persian. (Daniel 6: 25-28)

Darius, like Nebuchadnezzar before him, needed to learn that human kings could not order people to fear and revere the true and living God. Yet one can understand his excitement. He trusted in the LORD Jesus and received salvation and he wanted all his subjects to do the same. He wanted everyone in his kingdom to be part of Christ's eternal kingdom. Once a hater of God and His people, Darius now proclaimed a deep gratitude for his underserved salvation. He was amazed that the Most High should lavish His love upon him, and wanted to testify to His Saviour among all the nations of the world so that more people would follow the LORD.

By God's grace, a persecutor had become an evangelist. In God's sovereignty, an act of persecution led to the growth of His Church.

CHAPTER NINE

PROTECTING THE CHURCH FROM PERSECUTION

Members of your congregation are being attacked by adherents of a religion: some have had their houses set on fire; stones have been thrown at others; a few have been beaten to death.

Will the police, army, courts offer any help? Does your government give any protection to Christians? Probably not if that government is itself hostile to the LORD Jesus Christ; if it promotes a state religion or if the country's ruler regards himself as God. As we have seen, Christians are not safe in countries run by such governments. Those rulers offer no source of protection for local churches; they are the ones doing the persecution.

But in other countries, Christians are protected from persecution – the police stop violence against them; the courts punish those who attack them; the government ensures that there is no bias in the laws of the land against Christians.

Such governments are fulfilling the will of the Triune God by protecting His people. Some may consciously be seeking to serve Him; others may in fact serve other gods, but God the Father, Son and Holy Spirit uses those rulers for His purposes.

This chapter studies the way the Triune God worked through the kings of Persia to bring His people back from exile to Jerusalem and provide protection for them there. It demonstrates once again the sovereign power of the true and living God over the world and His love for His Church. The Scriptures under the spotlight are the books of Ezra, Haggai and Zechariah.

The Return from Exile

Prior to the Church being taken to Babylon, the Triune God had promised that He would bring it back from its exile. He had even given the date of its return. He used Gentile kings to remove the people from Judah; now He did the same to bring His people back to Judah.

In the first year of Cyrus king of Persia, in order to fulfil the word of the Lord spoken by Jeremiah, the Lord moved the heart of Cyrus king of Persia to make a proclamation throughout his realm and also to put it in writing:

This is what Cyrus king of Persia says:
"'The Lord, the God of heaven, has given me all the kingdoms of the earth and he has appointed me to build a temple for him at Jerusalem in Judah. Any of his people among you may go up to Jerusalem in Judah and build the temple of the Lord, the God of Israel, the God who is in Jerusalem, and may their God be with them. And in any locality where survivors may now be living, the people are to provide them with silver and gold, with goods and livestock, and with freewill offerings for the temple of God in Jerusalem.'"

> Then the family heads of Judah and Benjamin, and the priests and Levites – everyone whose heart God had moved – prepared to go up and build the house of the Lord in Jerusalem. (Ezra 1: 1-5)

God the Father, Son and Holy Spirit wanted His people to return to Judah – to rebuild His temple. He wanted Jerusalem to be a witness again to the Messiah; once more sacrifices would be performed which looked forward to the LORD Jesus. It had been promised long ago that the Messiah was to be an Israelite – from the tribe of Judah[1]. The Messiah was to be born in Judah.[2] So the Israelites had to return to Judah.

God's purpose in bringing His people back from exile was entirely to do with the saving work of the Messiah.

The Israelites who set off from Jerusalem had no political ambitions – in the sense that it was not their purpose to conquer the nations inhabiting the land; to regain what was 'theirs' by right; or to create their own powerful state. They had no political leader. Their King was *the* King – the Anointed One, the eternal Son of God. The Israelites returned to Jerusalem in order to be obedient to Him – to build His temple in order to witness to the Messiah.

Work commences

Once back in Jerusalem, the Israelites started the building work:

> When the seventh month came and the Israelites had settled in their towns, the people assembled together as one in Jerusalem. Then Joshua son of Jozadak and his

---

1   Genesis 49: 8-12

2   Micah 5: 2

fellow priests and Zerubbabel son of Shealtiel and his associates began to build the altar of the God of Israel to sacrifice burnt offerings on it, in accordance with what is written in the Law of Moses the man of God. Despite their fear of the peoples around them, they built the altar on its foundation and sacrificed burnt offerings on it to the Lord, both the morning and evening sacrifices. (Ezra 3: 1-3).

The Church came together as one body in Jerusalem to build the temple, starting with the altar and the foundation of the House. The people must have drawn strength from their unity; yet they were clearly worried also about the reaction of 'the peoples around them' to their building work. They felt vulnerable as they proclaimed their faith in the LORD Jesus in their new home. *What would their neighbours make of these 'newcomers' and the sacrifices they made in anticipation of the Messiah? Would the peoples want to worship Him also or would they scoff at Him and seek to persecute them? Would they seek to ban their worship of the LORD as the pagan kings of Babylon had tried to do? Would the peoples seek to eradicate them from the land?*

All such concerns were understandable but 'despite their fear of the peoples around them', the Israelites commenced the building work and reinstituted the morning and evening sacrifices. Each day at dawn and dusk they fed on Christ, as they sacrificed a lamb and offered oil-soaked bread and wine to the LORD.

What a glorious moment it must have been as they watched the blood fall from the animals and the dead bodies burn in the fire! It reminded them that the blood of the Messiah was shed for them. All their lust, anger, hatred and lies were eradicated because of THAT sacrifice – all burnt up in Christ's body. Nothing could separate them from the Triune God because of Christ. Through His Sacrifice they could relate to God Most High. There was no reason for them to be fearful of anything, however scared they must have felt returning to Israel, however vulnerable to enemy attack. They could have confidence that He would help them with their building work, whatever the peoples around them tried to do to them.

Keeping their eyes fixed on the blood of the Messiah helped the Church to remain focused on its task of proclaiming the Messiah.

The Israelites gradually reinstated the signs which pointed to the LORD Jesus Christ 'in accordance with what is written in the Law of Moses' (verse 4) – the priests, the Festival of Tabernacles, regular burnt offerings, the New Moon sacrifices and the sacrifices for all the appointed sacred festivals of the LORD, and the freewill offerings to the LORD. And as the foundation of the temple was laid, the people burst out 'with praise and thanksgiving' because of the LORD, the true Temple, and through whom they could be in fellowship with the true and living God: 'He is good; His love towards Israel endures for ever' (verse 11).

Opposition

As noted in previous chapters, any work of the Church which was about the Messiah was likely to face opposition. So it was no surprise that the Israelites experienced such persecution once they started to rebuild the temple.

> When the enemies of Judah and Benjamin heard that the exiles were building a temple for the LORD, the God of

Israel, they came to Zerubbabel and to the heads of the families and said, 'Let us help you build because, like you, we seek your God and have been sacrificing to him since the time of Esarhaddon king of Assyria, who brought us here.' (Ezra 4: 1-2).

It may seem paradoxical to read that the enemies of Judah had been making sacrifices to the God of Israel. The Scriptures record that those brought into the land by the king of Assyria during the time of the exile had indeed paid homage to the God of Israel. But, we are told, 'they also served their own gods in accordance with the customs of the nations from which they had been brought' (2 Kings 17: 33). To these peoples, the God of Israel was just one of many divine beings to whom they offered sacrifices, hoping to receive a blessing from some or all of them. They were open to all gods. Inevitably, therefore, they were hostile to the truth that only those who trust in the LORD Jesus are saved and can relate to the one true God: the LORD, the LORD, the Spirit of the LORD who is the One God. They stumbled on Christ the Rock.[3]

These peoples were not one with the LORD Jesus and His people. Hence, Ezra writes (v1), they were the 'enemies of Judah and Benjamin'. And their tactic for undermining the work of the Church was to try and join in with it: to disrupt it by being part of it. They sought to join the Church for the reason of promoting their own agenda within it. But the elders of the Church were wise to the danger[4]:

---

3   Isaiah 28: 16, Psalm 118:22, Isaiah 8:14 (see also Romans 10: 5-13, 1 Peter 2: 4-8).

4   One assumes that they had first enquired of the LORD about the issue (unlike when Israel was deceived by outsiders – see Joshua 9).

> Zerubbabel, Joshua and the rest of the heads of the families of Israel answered, 'You have no part with us in building a temple to our God. We alone will build it for the LORD, the God of Israel, as King Cyrus, the king of Persia, commanded us.' (Ezra 4: 3).

The elders made clear that their work was ordained by the LORD. And it had political authority. They were acting under the protection of the king of Persia. If anyone was going to oppose their work they needed to take it up with him. But the elders' refusal to allow the surrounding peoples to join the work served only to bring out into the open the true nature of their opposition to the Church:

> Then the peoples around them set out to discourage the people of Judah and make them afraid to go on building. They bribed officials to work against them and frustrate their plans during the entire reign of Cyrus king of Persia and down to the reign of Darius king of Persia. (Ezra 4: 4-5).

As so often in history, the enemies of the Church sought to use the state to oppose its gospel work; giving money to officials to slander and undermine the followers of the LORD Jesus.

Apathy

The passage above from Ezra chapter 4 tells us that the enemies of the Church sought to frustrate its plans to build the temple 'during the entire reign of Cyrus king of Persia and down to the reign of Darius king of Persia'. Later in Ezra we are told that 'the work on the house of God in Jerusalem came to a standstill until the second year of the reign of Darius king of Persia' (Ezra 4: 24).[5] Was this because of the opposition? Did the persecution become so intense that the work had to cease altogether?

A little digging into the Scriptures makes clear that this was not the case. Ezra tells us that the building work resumed (in the second year of the reign of Darius) when:

> Haggai the prophet and Zechariah the prophet, a descendant of Iddo, prophesied to the Jews in Judah and Jerusalem in the name of the God of Israel, who was over them. Then Zerubbabel son of Shealtiel and Joshua son of Jozadak set to work to rebuild the house of God in Jerusalem. And the prophets of God were with them, supporting them. (Ezra 5: 1-2)

The building work resumed through the encouragement of the prophets Haggai and Zechariah, and it becomes clear, when reading their prophecies, that the reason why the Church had stopped building the temple in Jerusalem in the first place was because of the people's *apathy*. It was not the Church's enemies who had halted its work. The Church itself had stopped work. And its opposition had ceased too. The followers of Christ rarely face much opposition from the world if they live like the world. And that, Haggai said, was exactly the problem of the Israelites:

> 'These people say, "The time has not yet come to rebuild the Lord's house."'

---

5   Ezra 4: 5-23 highlights some examples of opposition to the building work which took place later than the reign of Cyrus.

> Then the word of the Lord came through the prophet Haggai: 'Is it a time for you yourselves to be living in your panelled houses, while this house remains a ruin?'
>
> Now this is what the Lord Almighty says: 'Give careful thought to your ways. You have planted much but harvested little. You eat, but never have enough. You drink, but never have your fill. You put on clothes but are not warm. You earn wages, only to put them in a purse with holes in it.' (Haggai 1: 2-6)

The LORD made clear through Haggai that the people were too busy chasing the pleasures of the world to focus on building the temple – the witness to the work of the Messiah. Their hearts were focused on building a comfortable life for themselves, not seeking to do the LORD's work in response to His future sacrifice for their salvation. They were toiling to make their own homes look nice: converting their lofts; putting in new kitchens, repainting their bedrooms; laying new patios; mowing their lawns. And meanwhile the temple lay in ruins. And it would stay that way if the Church wasn't prepared to do the LORD's work.

The unwillingness of the Church to serve the LORD Jesus was a far greater hindrance to the proclamation of the Messiah than the attacks of its enemies.

Gospel Vision

The task given to Haggai and Zechariah by the LORD was to call the people to repent and turn back to Him:

> Then Zerubbabel son of Shealtiel, Joshua son of Jozadak, the high priest, and the whole remnant of the people obeyed the voice of the Lord their God and the

message of the prophet Haggai, because the Lord their God had sent him. And the people feared the Lord.

Then Haggai, the Lord's messenger, gave this message of the Lord to the people: 'I am with you,' declares the Lord. So the Lord stirred up the spirit of Zerubbabel son of Shealtiel, governor of Judah, and the spirit of Joshua son of Jozadak, the high priest, and the spirit of the whole remnant of the people. They came and began to work on the house of the Lord Almighty, their God, on the twenty-fourth day of the sixth month. (Haggai 1: 12-15)[6]

The Spirit of the LORD stirred up the people and, as they resumed their labour, the Triune God continued to encourage them. Even when the building work looked like it had achieved little, He wanted them to know that they should not be disheartened:

Be strong, Zerubbabel," declares the LORD. "Be strong, Joshua son of Jozadak, the high priest. Be strong, all you people of the land," declares the LORD, "and work. For I am with you," declares the LORD Almighty. "This is what I covenanted with you when you came out of Egypt. And my Spirit remains among you. Do not fear." (Haggai 2: 4-5)

The people had no need to fear those who might scorn or oppose them because the LORD was with them. He was the One who had accompanied them out of Egypt; He was in fellowship with them through His Spirit. Through the Spirit and the LORD Jesus Christ they intimately knew and loved God the Father. And the LORD urged them to rely on the power of His Spirit as they carried out their work on the temple:

---

6   See also Zechariah 1: 1-6

> This is the word of the Lord to Zerubbabel: "Not by might nor by power, but by my Spirit," says the Lord Almighty. 'What are you, mighty mountain? Before Zerubbabel you will become level ground. Then he will bring out the capstone to shouts of "God bless it! God bless it!"'

> Then the word of the Lord came to me: 'The hands of Zerubbabel have laid the foundation of this temple; his hands will also complete it. Then you will know that the Lord Almighty has sent me to you. Who dares despise the day of small things, since the seven eyes of the Lord that range throughout the earth will rejoice when they see the chosen capstone in the hand of Zerubbabel?' (Zechariah 4:6-10)

The building of the temple was not a demonstration of the might of the Israelites. Israel had never been chosen because of their power or righteousness[7]. And now, back from exile in Jerusalem, they were a rabble, with no human king, surrounded by hostile nations, building a small-scale temple lacking the glory of Solomon's creation. Yet none of that mattered if the LORD was with them. They were His people. They may have looked insignificant in the world's eyes. All the action seemed to be happening in the other more powerful nations. And yet the fate of the world lay within Israel. History revolved around them. Why? Because of their relation to the Messiah.

Haggai and Zechariah constantly sought to focus the hearts and minds of the people on the Messiah when encouraging them to resume the building work. They prophesied both His first and second coming – the key

---

7   See Deuteronomy 8-9.

moments of history. Through them, the Angel of the LORD promised that the LORD Almighty was to send Him to take flesh and dwell among them:

> I will live among you and you will know that the Lord Almighty has sent me to you (Zechariah 2: 11).[8]

The name of the Saviour was Joshua – or Jesus.

> Tell [Joshua] this is what the LORD Almighty says: "Here is the man whose name is the Branch, and he will branch out from his place and build the temple of the LORD. It is he who will build the temple of the LORD, and he will be clothed with majesty and will sit and rule on his throne. And he will be a priest on his throne. (Zechariah 6: 12-13)[9]

The Servant King would come and destroy the power of the Church's enemies:

> Rejoice greatly, Daughter Zion!
>   Shout, Daughter Jerusalem!
> See, your king comes to you,
>   righteous and victorious,
> lowly and riding on a donkey,
>   on a colt, the foal of a donkey.
> I will take away the chariots from Ephraim
>   and the war-horses from Jerusalem,
>   and the battle-bow will be broken.
> He will proclaim peace to the nations.

---

8   See also Zechariah 2: 8-9 on which Matthew Henry comments: *'The angel that talked with* the prophet (that is, Jesus Christ) tells him what he had commission to do for their protection and the perfecting of their salvation, and herein he has an eye to the great redemption which, in the fullness of time, he was to be the author of. Christ, who is Jehovah, and the Lord of hosts, of all the hosts of heaven and earth, in both which he has a sovereign power, *says,* He (that is, the Father) *has sent me', op cit, 1571*

9   See also Zechariah 3.

> His rule will extend from sea to sea
> and from the River to the ends of the earth.
> As for you, because of the blood of my covenant with you,
> I will free your prisoners from the waterless pit.
> (Zechariah 10: 9-11)

And this Servant would die to bring the salvation of the world.

> I will pour out on the house of David and the inhabitants of Jerusalem a spirit of grace and supplication. They will look on me, the one they have pierced, and they will mourn for him as one mourns for an only child, and grieve bitterly for him as one grieves for a firstborn son.
> (Zechariah 12: 10)

Furthermore, there would be another Day when the LORD Jesus would be sent by His Father to take away His enemies and institute a new creation for His people:

> Then the LORD will appear over them;
> his arrow will flash like lightning.
> The Sovereign LORD will sound the trumpet;
> he will march in the storms of the south,
> and the LORD Almighty will shield them.
> They will destroy
> and overcome with slingstones.
> They will drink and roar as with wine;
> they will be full like a bowl
> used for sprinkling the corners of the altar.
> The LORD their God will save his people on that day
> as a shepherd saves his flock.
> They will sparkle in his land
> like jewels in a crown.
> (Zechariah 10: 14-16)

The LORD's people were urged to look forward to the time when all the wicked would be defeated, and the LORD Jesus would reign supreme:

> The LORD will be king over the whole earth. On that day there will be one LORD, and His name the only name. (Zechariah 14: 9)

The fate of Israel and the temple looked precarious in Jerusalem; yet, the LORD said, His people had a glorious future. It was the rest of the nations whose future was under threat. For He promised that:

> In a little while I will once more shake the heavens and the earth, the sea and the dry land. I will shake all nations, and what is desired by all nations will come, and I will fill this house with glory," says the LORD Almighty. "The silver is mine and the gold is mine," declares the LORD Almighty. "The glory of this present house will be greater than the glory of the former house," says the LORD Almighty. "And in this place I will grant peace," declares the LORD Almighty.

> I am going to shake the heavens and earth. I will overturn royal thrones and shatter the power of the foreign kingdoms. I will overthrow chariots and their drivers; horses and their riders will fall, each by the sword of his brother' (Haggai 2: 6-9, 21-22).

The Person who is 'desired by all nations' – *the* Desired of all nations – was to come and fill the temple with glory. The Messiah was coming[10]. Although His Kingdom might appear oppressed, it would destroy all the political kingdoms of the

---

10   The promise to Zerubbabel in Haggai 2: 20-22 is a promise that the Messiah – who is the signet on God's right hand – will be one of his descendants. Thus Zerubbabel was given the promise which had been taken from his forefather, Jehoiachin (Jeremiah 22: 24-30) continuing the line of David to the Messiah (see 2 Samuel 7: 11-16, Matthew 1: 12-13).

world. They would crumble; the Kingdom would endure forever. What can be shaken will be removed 'so that what cannot be shaken may remain'[11]. Robert Jamieson comments:

> The transitoriness of all that is earthly should lead men to seek "peace" in Messiah's everlasting kingdom (Hag 2:9; Heb 12:27, 28). The Jews in Haggai's times hesitated about going forward with the work, through dread of the world power, Medo-Persia, influenced by the craft of Samaria. The prophet assures them this and all other world powers are to fall before Messiah, who is to be associated with this temple; therefore they need fear naught.[12]

Work resumes

The prophecies of the Messiah given by Haggai and Zechariah encouraged the Church to resume work on the temple in Jerusalem (Ezra 5: 1-2). Their desire to build the great witness to the Messiah was rekindled. Rather than focus on their own wealth and happiness, they wanted to hold up the Name of Christ to the world. Yet as the Church restarted its work on the temple so the opposition to them resumed:

> At that time Tattenai, governor of Trans-Euphrates, and Shethar-Bozenai and their associates went to them and asked, 'Who authorised you to rebuild this temple and to finish it?' They also asked, 'What are the names of those who are constructing this building?' But the eye of their God was watching over the elders of the Jews, and they were not stopped until a report could go to Darius and his written reply be received. (Ezra 5: 3-5).

---

11 See Hebrews 12: 25-29 – commenting on Haggai 2. The heavens and earth shake through both the first and second coming of the Messiah.

12 Jamieson, Robert, [1871] *Commentary Critical and Explanatory on the Whole Bible* [Online} Available at https://www.ccel.org/ccel/jamieson/jfb.x.xxxvii.iii.html#x.xxxvii.iii-p0.1 [2019, January]

Those obsessed by human power want all of life to be under their control in some fashion. The rulers of Trans-Euphrates sought – in a typical bureaucratic, humourless fashion – to stop the building of the temple by questioning whether it had any political authority. However, a much greater authority – the God of Israel – was looking over them. He enabled the work to continue whilst the debate about its legitimacy was subject to correspondence with King Darius, which went as follows:

This is the letter which the Trans-Euphrates' rulers wrote:

To King Darius:

Cordial greetings.

The king should know that we went to the district of Judah, to the temple of the great God. The people are building it with large stones and placing the timbers in the walls. The work is being carried on with diligence and is making rapid progress under their direction.

We questioned the elders and asked them, 'Who authorised you to rebuild this temple and to finish it?' We also asked them their names, so that we could write down the names of their leaders for your information.

This is the answer they gave us: 'We are the servants of the God of heaven and earth, and we are rebuilding the temple that was built many years ago, one that a great king of Israel built and finished. But because our ancestors angered the God of heaven, he gave them into the hands of Nebuchadnezzar the Chaldean, king of Babylon, who destroyed this temple and deported the people to Babylon.

'However, in the first year of Cyrus king of Babylon, King Cyrus issued a decree to rebuild this house of God. He even removed from the temple of Babylon the gold and silver articles of the house of God, which Nebuchadnezzar had taken from the temple in Jerusalem and brought to the temple in Babylon. Then King Cyrus gave them to a man named Sheshbazzar, whom he had appointed governor, and he told him, "Take these articles and go and deposit them in the temple in Jerusalem. And rebuild the house of God on its site."

'So this Sheshbazzar came and laid the foundations of the house of God in Jerusalem. From that day to the present it has been under construction but is not yet finished.'

Now if it pleases the king, let a search be made in the royal archives of Babylon to see if King Cyrus did in fact issue a decree to rebuild this house of God in Jerusalem. Then let the king send us his decision in this matter. (Ezra 5: 7-17).

The Israelites made clear under whose authority they were acting – 'We are the servants of the God of heaven and earth'. It was *His* temple they were rebuilding. And yet they also keen to highlight the political authority they possessed for their building work. It had been the subject of a decree by king Cyrus. They were carrying out his orders. The people did not invest faith in him. Yet they respected the authority of the king – first Cyrus; now Darius. And they sought his protection from those seeking to oppose their work on the temple of the Messiah.

Back in Babylon, Darius ordered his civil servants into action, and they found the relevant memorandum which proved that king Cyrus had indeed issued a decree authorising the re-building of the temple of God in Jerusalem.[13] And so Darius wrote:

---

13   Ezra 6: 1-5.

Now then, Tattenai, governor of Trans-Euphrates, and Shethar-Bozenai and you other officials of that province, stay away from there. Do not interfere with the work on this temple of God. Let the governor of the Jews and the Jewish elders rebuild this house of God on its site.

Moreover, I hereby decree what you are to do for these elders of the Jews in the construction of this house of God:

Their expenses are to be fully paid out of the royal treasury, from the revenues of Trans-Euphrates, so that the work will not stop. Whatever is needed – young bulls, rams, male lambs for burnt offerings to the God of heaven, and wheat, salt, wine and olive oil, as requested by the priests in Jerusalem – must be given them daily without fail, so that they may offer sacrifices pleasing to the God of heaven and pray for the well-being of the king and his sons.

Furthermore, I decree that if anyone defies this edict, a beam is to be pulled from their house and they are to be impaled on it. And for this crime their house is to be made a pile of rubble. May God, who has caused his Name to dwell there, overthrow any king or people who lifts a hand to change this decree or to destroy this temple in Jerusalem.

I Darius have decreed it. Let it be carried out with diligence. (Ezra 6: 6-12).

The rulers of Trans-Euphrates had sought to use constitutional means to curtail the work of the Church; yet the same means not only served to protect the Church, they forced the rulers to actively help the Jews!

Because of the decree King Darius had sent, Tattenai, governor of Trans-Euphrates, and Shethar-Bozenai and their associates carried it out with diligence. So the elders of the Jews continued to build and prosper under the preaching of Haggai the prophet and Zechariah, a descendant of Iddo. They finished building the temple according to the command of the God of Israel and the decrees of Cyrus, Darius and Artaxerxes, kings of Persia. The temple was completed on the third day of the month Adar, in the sixth year of the reign of King Darius. (Ezra 6: 6-12).

The King and kings

The temple was completed; once more there was a building in Jerusalem proclaiming the saving work of the Messiah. The labour was provided by the Israelites; Cyrus, Darius, and Artaxerxes provided them with protection and practical assistance. It was the Church's job to proclaim the gospel of Christ; and it was the responsibility of political rulers to provide the Church with the freedom and safety to do its gospel work. And that was exactly what Cyrus, Darius, and Artaxerxes did in supporting the Israelites in rebuilding the temple, and later the walls of Jerusalem. Ezra himself returned from exile under the protection of Artaxerxes. And so Ezra gave praise to:

> The Lord, the God of our ancestors, who has put it into the king's heart to bring honour to the house of the Lord in Jerusalem in this way and who has extended his good favour to me before the king and his advisors and all the king's powerful officials (Ezra 7: 27-28).[14]

The Church itself needed no king; it had its own King, the true King, the Son of God who is 'the most exalted of the

---

14 Artaxerxes had a little hiccup in his support of Israel when he was persuaded to order the cessation of the work on the rebuilding of Jerusalem (after the temple was completed) (see Ezra 4: 6-23). But subsequently he was as supportive as Cyrus and Darius (see Ezra 7: 11-28 and Nehemiah 2: 1-9 and 13: 6-7).

kings of the earth'[15]. But the Triune God raised up kings to protect His Church. They too were His servants. Some were faithful, and the Bible praises the assistance they gave to the Church: e.g. Pharaoh protecting Joseph and the family of Israel in Egypt[16]; Hiram king of Tyre helping Solomon to build the temple[17].

Other kings, however, are condemned by the Holy Spirit for not helping the Church or attacking it. For example, all the kings who did not provide assistance to Israel as they travelled to the Promised Land: the kings of Edom and Moab[18], Sihon king of the Amorites and Og king of Bashan, all of whom prevented the Israelites safe passage through the desert.[19] Some of the nations were cursed for their hostile attitude to the Church:

> No Ammonite or Moabite or any of their descendants may enter the assembly of the Lord, not even in the tenth generation. For they did not come to meet you with bread and water on your way when you came out of Egypt, and they hired Balaam son of Beor from Pethor in Aram Naharaim to pronounce a curse on you (Numbers 23: 3-4)

Likewise some nations were cursed for their gloating attitude to Israel when it was exiled from the land.

> Because of the violence done to your brother Jacob, shame shall cover you, and you shall be cut off forever. On the day that you stood aloof, on the day that strangers carried off his wealth and foreigners entered his gates

---

15   Psalm 89: 27. It is worth noting that the Israelites did not seek a king on return to Jerusalem.

16   Genesis 41-47.

17   1 Kings 5

18   Numbers 20: 14-21, Judges 11: 16-17.

19   Numbers 21

and cast lots for Jerusalem, you were like one of them. But do not gloat over the day of your brother in the day of his misfortune; do not rejoice over the people of Judah in the day of their ruin; do not boast in the day of distress. (Obadiah 1: 10-12)[20]

Truly the LORD blesses those who bless His people; curses those who curse them[21]. 'Whoever touches you touches the apple of His eye' (Zechariah 2: 8). Such was the love of the LORD for His people – the love that meant He was prepared to die for them.

Little wonder then that the people celebrated the re-building of the temple by joyfully offering sacrifices to the LORD Jesus in anticipation of the Sacrifice of the Messiah, who is the Passover Lamb:

Then the people of Israel – the priests, the Levites and the rest of the exiles – celebrated the dedication of the house of God with joy. For the dedication of this house of God they offered a hundred bulls, two hundred rams, four hundred male lambs and, as a sin offering for all Israel, twelve male goats, one for each of the tribes of Israel. And they installed the priests in their divisions and the Levites in their groups for the service of God at Jerusalem, according to what is written in the Book of Moses.

On the fourteenth day of the first month, the exiles celebrated the Passover. The priests and Levites had purified themselves and were all ceremonially clean. The Levites slaughtered the Passover lamb for all the exiles, for their relatives the priests and for themselves. So the Israelites who had returned from the exile ate it, together

---

20   See also Ezekiel 25, 35, 36: 1-7.

21   Genesis 12: 3.

with all who had separated themselves from the unclean practices of their Gentile neighbours in order to seek the Lord, the God of Israel. For seven days they celebrated with joy the Festival of Unleavened Bread, because the Lord had filled them with joy by changing the attitude of the king of Assyria so that he assisted them in the work on the house of God, the God of Israel (Ezra 6: 16-22).

The Israelites proclaimed their faith in the LORD Jesus and as they did so, Gentiles joined them in their celebrations. As Matthew Henry comments, the Gentiles:

separated themselves from the filthiness of sin and fellowship with sinners, joined themselves with the Israel of God in conformity and communion, and set themselves to seek the God of Israel; and those that do so in sincerity, though strangers and foreigners, are welcome to eat of the gospel feast, as fellow-citizens with the saints and of the household of God.[22]

This fulfilled the promised the LORD had made through Zechariah that 'Many nations will be joined with the LORD... and will become my people' (2: 11)

The Church (native born Jews and Gentile converts) gathered in Jerusalem to worship the LORD, waiting for the Messiah to come.

---

22   Matthew Henry, op cit, 621

CHAPTER TEN

———————

PERSECUTION OF THE KING

The preceding chapters have studied some examples
of the persecution of the Old Testament prophets,
who trusted in the LORD Jesus Christ and looked
forward to His future work of salvation. They suffered
because of their testimony to Jesus.

This chapter looks at the first-hand accounts given
in the Gospels of the way that Jesus fulfilled all that
the prophets had said would happen to Him – His
suffering and glory.

The King arrives

A few centuries after the temple was rebuilt in Jerusalem,
the Messiah was born in Israel. The Word became flesh. The
Passover Lamb had arrived – the One who was to take away
the sin of the world; the One about whom Moses and the
prophets wrote – Jesus of Nazareth, the son of Joseph.[1]

The arrival of the Messiah had long been prophesied; as
had the fact that He would be persecuted when He did
come to Israel. So it was no surprise that His life was under
threat from birth. The persecution of the Church throughout
the ages, right back to the time of Abel, was driven by
Satan's desire to eliminate the prophesied Seed of the

———————
1   See John 1

Woman, the Son of God.[2] It was inevitable that when the Seed of the Woman arrived, He should face persecution:

'When [the Magi] had gone, an angel of the Lord appeared to Joseph in a dream. 'Get up,' he said, 'take the child and his mother and escape to Egypt. Stay there until I tell you, for Herod is going to search for the child to kill him.'

So he got up, took the child and his mother during the night and left for Egypt, where he stayed until the death of Herod. And so was fulfilled what the Lord had said through the prophet: 'Out of Egypt I called my son.' [Hosea 11:1]

When Herod realised that he had been outwitted by the Magi, he was furious, and he gave orders to kill all the boys in Bethlehem and its vicinity who were two years old and under, in accordance with the time he had learned from the Magi. (Matthew 2: 13-16)

Later when the LORD started His public ministry, the devil immediately sought to tempt Him away from His calling and destroy His ministry. Christ resisted the various enticements offered to Him; yet Satan did not give up: 'When the devil had finished all this tempting, he left [Christ] until an opportune time'[3].

Satan's greatest allies in seeking to harm the LORD were the religious authorities in Israel. They were blind to the teaching of the Law and Prophets about the need to trust in Christ[4]; they sought to find salvation through their own righteous acts. Salvation was about *them*. Thus they were

---

2   Genesis 3: 16, Galatians 4: 4

3   Luke 4: 13; see 1-13.

4   John 1: 45, 5: 39, Matthew 5: 17, 11: 13; Luke 24: 44;

angered to hear Christ teach from the Scriptures that they needed to look to *Him* for the forgiveness of sins[5]; that eternal life was found in *Him*; and that without *Him* they were unclean[6]. They were offended by the truth that there was nothing anyone could or needed to do to earn the gift of salvation: that they just needed to humbly trust in Jesus as their LORD and turn away from being lord of their own lives.

But to trust in Jesus was gravely injurious to the pride of the religious Israelites. Like Cain, they thought God was pleased with the goodness of their works. They believed they could relate to God without Christ as Mediator. Hence they did not merely resist Jesus; they hated Him and wanted to destroy Him. So obsessed were they by the need to earn their salvation through their good works that they persecuted the LORD for healing someone on the Sabbath, for daring to demonstrate that He was the LORD of the Sabbath[7] who could drive out disease and decay and usher in the new creation:

> Another time Jesus went into the synagogue, and a man with a shrivelled hand was there. Some of them were looking for a reason to accuse Jesus, so they watched him closely to see if he would heal him on the Sabbath. Jesus said to the man with the shrivelled hand, 'Stand up in front of everyone.'
>
> Then Jesus asked them, 'Which is lawful on the Sabbath: to do good or to do evil, to save life or to kill?' But they remained silent.

5   Matthew 9: 1-8.

6   Matthew 9: 10-13, 15: 1-20; 23: 1-39

7   Matthew 12: 1-14

> He looked around at them in anger and, deeply distressed at their stubborn hearts, said to the man, 'Stretch out your hand.' He stretched it out, and his hand was completely restored. Then the Pharisees went out and began to plot with the Herodians how they might kill Jesus. (Mark 3: 1-6)

Seeking their own righteousness, the religious leaders wanted to be lords of their lives (and of their fellow Jews). They would not accept Christ as LORD – that He was the Son of God.

> So, because Jesus was doing these things on the Sabbath, the Jewish leaders began to persecute him. In his defence Jesus said to them, 'My Father is always at his work to this very day, and I too am working.' For this reason they tried all the more to kill him; not only was he breaking the Sabbath, but he was even calling God his own Father, making himself equal with God. (John 5: 16-18)[8]

The LORD Jesus threatened the hold that the religious authorities had over the Jewish nation. They believed that *they* should determine who was – and who was not – a proper Jew. When Jesus showed up saying that anyone – even 'sinners' – could enter the Kingdom by faith in Him, they feared that they would lose their authority. They would lose their religious power – and put at risk their political agenda to rule Israel:

> Many of the Jews who had come to visit Mary, and had seen what Jesus did [the healing of Lazarus], believed in him. But some of them went to the Pharisees and told them what Jesus had done. Then the chief priests and the Pharisees called a meeting of the Sanhedrin.

---

8   See also John 10: 22-33.

'What are we accomplishing?' they asked. 'Here is this man performing many signs. If we let him go on like this, everyone will believe in him, and then the Romans will come and take away both our temple and our nation.' (John 11: 45-48)

Now the crowd that was with him when he called Lazarus from the tomb and raised him from the dead continued to spread the word. Many people, because they had heard that he had performed this sign, went out to meet him. So the Pharisees said to one another, 'See, this is getting us nowhere. Look how the whole world has gone after him!' (John 12: 17-19)[9]

Relentless Persecution

The Pharisees and the teachers of the Law led the charge to get rid of the LORD Jesus. But He faced attack from many quarters. He was persecuted in his home town by those refusing to accept He was the Son of God[10]. Some of those who became His disciples grumbled when He offered them eternal life, and deserted Him.[11] Many of the Jews would not accept that Jesus was the God of Abraham and Moses:

[Jesus said] Very truly I tell you, whoever obeys my word will never see death.'

At this [the Jews who had believed Jesus] exclaimed, 'Now we know that you are demon-possessed! Abraham died and so did the prophets, yet you say that whoever

---

9   See also Mark 11: 18 where after Jesus cleanses the Temple, by driving out the money-changers and salesmen, it is said that the chief priests and the teachers of the law 'began looking for a way to kill him, for they feared him, because the whole crowd was amazed at his teaching'.

10   Luke 4: 23-30

11   John 6: 25-66

obeys your word will never taste death. Are you greater than our father Abraham? He died, and so did the prophets. Who do you think you are?'

Jesus replied, 'If I glorify myself, my glory means nothing. My Father, whom you claim as your God, is the one who glorifies me. Though you do not know him, I know him. If I said I did not, I would be a liar like you, but I do know him and obey his word. Your father Abraham rejoiced at the thought of seeing my day; he saw it and was glad.'

'You are not yet fifty years old,' they said to him, 'and you have seen Abraham!'

'Very truly I tell you,' Jesus answered, 'before Abraham was born, I am!' At this, they picked up stones to stone him, but Jesus hid himself, slipping away from the temple grounds. (John 8: 51-59)

The LORD stood in the line of the prophets who came before Him: He was *the* Prophet to whom those prophets had witnessed[12]. As the prophets had been persecuted for proclaiming the gospel of Christ, so the LORD was persecuted for preaching the gospel about Himself. As He told those seeking His downfall:

Listen to another parable: there was a landowner who planted a vineyard. He put a wall round it, dug a winepress in it and built a watchtower. Then he rented the vineyard to some farmers and moved to another place. When the harvest time approached, he sent his servants to the tenants to collect his fruit.

The tenants seized his servants; they beat one, killed another, and stoned a third. Then he sent other servants

12   Deut. 18:15-19; John 6: 14, 7: 40; Acts 3:22-23

to them, more than the first time, and the tenants treated them in the same way. Last of all, he sent his son to them. "They will respect my son," he said.

But when the tenants saw the son, they said to each other, "This is the heir. Come, let's kill him and take his inheritance." So they took him and threw him out of the vineyard and killed him. (Matthew 21: 33-39)[13]

After telling this parable, Jesus pointed to the Scriptures to teach that those who did not trust in Him would be crushed.[14] Yet, even though the religious authorities knew Jesus was talking about them, they still wanted to silence Him: 'They looked for a way to arrest him, but they were afraid of the crowd because the people held that he was a prophet' (v46).

A Mission of Suffering

That Jesus experienced this persecution was not a surprise to Him. He understood that He had a mission of suffering from reading the Scriptures about Himself. The Scriptures record a few occasions when the Father talked directly to His Son[15]; most of the time, the Father spoke to Jesus as He read the Scriptures. And through the power of the Spirit, He understood that He was the subject of them. He testified, 'Here I am, I have come – it is written about me in the scroll.'[16] And He made clear to those who followed Him that the Scriptures were about Him.

---

13 See Jeremiah 7:25-26; 25: 4-6; 26: 4-6; 29: 19; 35: 15; 44: 4-6; Luke 13: 31-35, Matthew 13: 53-58, Acts 7: 52-53

14 Matthew 21: 42 quoting Psalm 118:22-23.

15 Matthew 3: 16-17, 17: 1-8, John 12: 27-33 (when the Father spoke for the disciples' benefit not Christ's).

16 Psalm 40: 7, Hebrews 10: 5-10, Matthew 5: 17

> You study the Scriptures diligently because you think that in them you have eternal life. These are the very Scriptures that testify about me, yet you refuse to come to me to have life.
>
> But do not think I will accuse you before the Father. Your accuser is Moses, on whom your hopes are set. If you believed Moses, you would believe me, for he wrote about me. But since you do not believe what he wrote, how are you going to believe what I say?'
> (John 5: 39-40, 45-47)
>
> He said to them, 'How foolish you are, and how slow to believe all that the prophets have spoken! Did not the Messiah have to suffer these things and then enter his glory?' And beginning with Moses and all the Prophets, he explained to them what was said in all the Scriptures concerning himself. (Luke 24: 25-27)[17]

The LORD Jesus knew from the Law and the Prophets that He *had* to die. He was the King of the Jews – King of the whole world. But He had not come as a political conqueror. He was a disappointment to those wanting a freedom fighter to liberate the Jews from the Romans:

> After the people saw the sign Jesus performed [feeding the 5000], they began to say, 'Surely this is the Prophet who is to come into the world.' Jesus, knowing that they intended to come and make him king by force, withdrew again to a mountain by himself. (John 6: 14-15)

The Prophet had indeed come – but His mission was not to conquer the Romans but to serve humanity by being killed by the Romans (aided by the religious authorities). This King

---

17   See also Luke 24: 44-47

was not obsessed with earthly power. Jesus made clear to His followers that one could not understand Him – and one could not know God at all – without acknowledging that it was His job to suffer:

> From that time on Jesus began to explain to his disciples that he must go to Jerusalem and suffer many things at the hands of the elders, the chief priests and the teachers of the law, and that he must be killed and on the third day be raised to life.
>
> Peter took him aside and began to rebuke him. 'Never, Lord!' he said. 'This shall never happen to you!'
>
> Jesus turned and said to Peter, 'Get behind me, Satan! You are a stumbling-block to me; you do not have in mind the concerns of God, but merely human concerns.' (Matthew 16: 21-23)

Those belonging to the world did not comprehend the LORD Jesus[18] – they had not understood what the Law and Prophets had foretold about Him:

> Jesus took the Twelve aside and told them, 'We are going up to Jerusalem, and everything that is written by the prophets about the Son of Man will be fulfilled. He will be handed over to the Gentiles. They will mock him, insult him and spit on him; they will flog him and kill him. On the third day he will rise again.' The disciples did not understand any of this. Its meaning was hidden from them, and they did not know what he was talking about. (Luke 18: 31-34)[19]

---

18   See also John 7: 1-9 (where Jesus' brothers express their desire for Him to become a public figure) and John 8: 21-30

19   See also Luke 24: 25-27

Enduring the Persecution

The LORD Jesus never once retaliated when He experienced persecution – when He was verbally or physically abused. He never sought to even the score when insults were thrown at him; never retaliated when attacked. He submitted to the suffering which He knew would lead to His death.[20] Yet He did not passively acquiesce to His suffering. He *positively* submitted to it. He did so out of strength not weakness.

How was the LORD Jesus Christ able to endure the persecution He experienced without fighting back against it?

First, Jesus knew His Father's love. He knew the truth of that love from the Scriptures and from the words and actions of His Father, to whom He was united through the Spirit. On the occasions when the Father spoke directly to Christ, He testified to His love for His Son. The LORD Jesus repeatedly proclaimed the Father's love for Him[21]. He knew, therefore, that His Father would protect Him in the face of His suffering, even though His closest followers would desert Him. 'I am not alone, for my Father is with me' (John 16: 32).

The LORD spent regular time with His Father, praying to Him for understanding and strength. On the occasions when He was most under pressure and most tired, He deliberately made the effort to have fellowship with His Father; to listen to Him and speak to Him:

> Very early in the morning, while it was still dark, Jesus got up, left the house and went off to a solitary place, where he prayed. (Mark 1: 35)

---

20   As one of His disciples commented, 'When they hurled their insults at him, he did not retaliate; when he suffered, he made no threats. Instead, he entrusted himself to him who judges justly'. (1 Peter 2: 23).

21   See, for example, John 3: 35; 5: 20; 10: 17; 15: 9.

> The news about Jesus spread even more, so that crowds of people came to hear him and to be healed of their sicknesses. But Jesus often withdrew to lonely places and prayed. (Luke 5: 15-16)

> Jesus went out to a mountainside to pray, and spent the night praying to God. (Luke 6: 12[22])

Through this fellowship with His Father, the LORD Jesus gained the strength to face the persecution He endured – especially as death approached:

> Then Jesus went with his disciples to a place called Gethsemane, and he said to them, 'Sit here while I go over there and pray.'... Going a little farther, he fell with his face to the ground and prayed... .Then he returned to his disciples and found them sleeping. 'Couldn't you men keep watch with me for one hour?' he asked Peter. 'Watch and pray so that you will not fall into temptation. The spirit is willing, but the flesh is weak.'
> (Matthew 26: 36, 40-41)

> During the days of Jesus' life on earth, he offered up prayers and petitions with fervent cries and tears to the one who could save him from death. (Hebrews 5: 7)

Second, Jesus desired to do His Father's will. The Father loved Him; and He loved His Father. As the LORD Jesus read the Scriptures, the Spirit helped Him to grow in wisdom and maturity[23]. He loved to read the Law and Prophets because He wanted to hear His Father speak; to know His will; and to *do* that will. His 'food' was to do the will of Him who sent Him.[24] Jesus fulfilled what the Scriptures had said about His attentiveness to His Father's will:

---

22   In this way, Christ fulfilled Psalm 119: 147-8 and 164

23   Luke 2: 40, 52

24   John 4:34

> Here I am, I have come – it is written about me in the
> scroll. **I desire to do your will, my God; your law is
> within my heart.'** (Psalm 40: 7-8[25])

The LORD did not merely hear His Father's words, He put
them into practice. He loved His Father and wanted to be
obedient to Him. For His Father's sake, He resisted the
devil and his enticements[26]. He followed His Father not the
evil one:

> I will not say much more to you, for the prince of this
> world is coming. He has no hold over me, but he comes
> so that the world may learn that I love the Father
> and do exactly what my Father has commanded me.
> (John 14: 30-31)

Christ knew that it was His Father's will 'to cause Him to
suffer'[27]. He did not face the cross fearing that the Father
had no knowledge of it or that it was outside His control.
And so, out of love for His Father, Christ overcame the
temptation to escape from the death that faced Him. Thus
when the LORD Jesus went with His disciples to pray in
Gethsemane, His sole concern was to do His Father's will:

> He fell with his face to the ground and prayed,
> 'My Father, if it is possible, may this cup be taken from
> me. Yet not as I will, but as you will.' He went away a
> second time and prayed, 'My Father, if it is not possible
> for this cup to be taken away unless I drink it, may your
> will be done.' When he came back, he again found them
> sleeping, because their eyes were heavy. So he left them

---

25   See Hebrews 10: 5-10

26   'See Luke 4: 1-13 cf Adam, the son of God, born without sin, who failed to
resist the devil and do the will of God (Genesis 3).

27   Isaiah 53: 10.

and went away once more and prayed the third time, saying the same thing. (Matthew 26: 39-44).[28]

After His incarnation, the LORD Jesus had a body, mind and spirit like any other human being. Yet unlike any other human, He was fully obedient to the Father. His obedience was not merely theoretical; it was intensely practical; it survived every test – 'even death on a cross'[29]. Having demonstrated His loving obedience to His Father and that He was without sin, Christ was fit to be the Righteous Sacrifice, the perfect Lamb of God[30]:

> During the days of Jesus' life on earth, he offered up prayers and petitions with fervent cries and tears to the one who could save him from death, and he was heard because of his reverent submission. Son though he was, he learned obedience from what he suffered and, once made perfect, he became the source of eternal salvation for all who obey him. (Hebrews 5: 7-9)[31]

Third, Jesus endured the persecution He suffered because He shared His Father's love for humanity and His anger at their sin. The Father and Spirit desperately wanted the Son to have a Bride. The Son wanted His Bride, the Church. Yet She had turned away from Him: following other gods; trusting in idols; living selfishly; 'filled with every

---

28   John 12: 27-28 – 'Now my soul is troubled, and what shall I say? "Father, save me from this hour"? No, it was for this very reason I came to this hour. Father, glorify your name!' Then a voice came from heaven, 'I have glorified it, and will glorify it again.'

29   Philippians 2: 8.

30   Isaiah 53:3-12; Hebrews 4: 15; 2 Corinthians 5: 21; 1 Peter 1: 19.

31   Hebrews 2: 10: 'In bringing many sons and daughters to glory, it was fitting that God, for whom and through whom everything exists, should make the pioneer of their salvation perfect through what he suffered'.

kind of wickedness, evil, greed and depravity'[32]. The world which the Father, Spirit and Son had created for the Son's Bride was dirty, contaminated by the sin of humanity.

But the Son still loved His Bride; and the Father and Spirit still yearned that His Bride should be His. It was because the Three Persons of God loved the Bride so much that the Three Persons of God were so angry at the evil in the world. God the Father, Son and Spirit yearned for the sin of His Bride to be atoned for and taken away – that She might be washed clean and have a perfect place in which to dwell.[33]

Christ so loved His Bride He was willing to be united to Her sin, to take Her shame upon Him; to lay down His life for her and take the punishment for Her transgressions so that She might be reconciled to the Triune God, through Him[34]. Christ was prepared to take upon Himself His wrath for humanity's sin – the wrath He shared with His Father and the Spirit.[35] There must be justice for all the damage humanity had caused to the world. A ransom was needed to pay for humanity's wickedness, to release them from their sins and restore their relationship with the Triune God. And it was Christ who paid the ransom (Matthew 20: 28), paying it to Himself and the Father and the Spirit.

The Father, Son and Spirit so loved the Bride that they were willing for the eternal loving relationship between the Three Persons of God to end. The Father was prepared to sacrifice the Son He loved; and Christ was prepared to *be* sacrificed.

---

32 Romans 1: 29.

33 Matthew 8: 10-12; 22: 1-14, 25: 31-46.

34 Isaiah 53:3-12

35 Jesus' hatred of sin is shown, for example, in Luke 15.

What love!

Because God (the Father) so loved the world, He gave His one and only Son... (John 3: 16)

This is love, not that we loved God, but that He loved us and sent His Son as an atoning sacrifice for our sins (1 John 4: 10).

[Jesus said] I am the good shepherd; I know my sheep and my sheep know me – just as the Father knows me and I know the Father – and I lay down my life for the sheep. I have other sheep that are not of this sheepfold. I must bring them also. They too will listen to my voice, and there shall be one flock and one shepherd. The reason my Father loves me is that I lay down my life – only to take it up again. No one takes it from me, but I lay it down of my own accord. I have authority to lay it down and authority to take it up again. This command I received from my Father.' (John 10: 14-18)

[Jesus said] As the Father has loved me, so have I loved you... Greater love has no one than this: to lay down one's life for one's friends. (John 15: 9, 13)

Fourth, Jesus endured His suffering knowing that glory would follow. He was to suffer and die but He knew also that His loving Father wanted Him to be delivered through death and be restored to relationship with Him. That had been prophesied long ago. 'Even though I walk through the darkest valley, I will fear no evil, for you are with me' (Psalm 23: 4).

Christ felt complete assurance in the face of His suffering because of His Father's love. He knew that after His suffering, there would be glory: the glory of the salvation He would bring to His Bride; victory over sin and death, eternal life; a new heaven and earth. He knew it was His Father's will that He would rise back to life; to be restored as the eternal Son of the Father and ascend to be with Him in heaven, with everything under His feet; and that one day He would return to earth to judge the living and the dead.[36]

Christ knew that it was His Father's will that the Son of Man must 'suffer many things and be rejected by this generation'; but He knew also that He would later arrive in glory like 'the lightning, which flashes and lights up the sky from one end to the other' (Luke 17: 24-25). The Son of Man would come again and rule over the world: casting out those who rejected Him and making the world fit for His Bride.[37]

The Final Hour

And so the hour came when the LORD must die. Satan's mission to destroy the Seed of the Woman came to fulfilment. He had the religious authorities on his side; next he enticed one of the disciples to betray Christ:

> Now the Festival of Unleavened Bread, called the Passover, was approaching, and the chief priests and the teachers of the law were looking for some way to get rid of Jesus, for they were afraid of the people. Then Satan entered Judas, called Iscariot, one of the Twelve. And Judas went to the chief priests and the officers of the temple guard and discussed with them how he might betray Jesus. They were delighted and agreed to give him money. He consented, and watched for an opportunity to hand Jesus over to them when no crowd was present. (Luke 22: 1-6)

36 See, for example, Matthew 16: 21, 13: 36-41, 19: 28-30, Luke 20: 21-24 and Mark 14: 62.

37 Matthew 13: 36-42, 19: 28-30; 22: 1-14.

Christ knew that Judas was to betray Him – that had also been prophesied long ago[38]. He did not resist arrest; He had not come to lead a rebellion against the worldly authorities. He submitted Himself to the evil of the authorities, knowing that it was His death that would undermine their power:

> Judas, one of the Twelve, appeared [in the Garden of Gethsemane]. With him was a crowd armed with swords and clubs, sent from the chief priests, the teachers of the law, and the elders.
>
> Now the betrayer had arranged a signal with them: 'The one I kiss is the man; arrest him and lead him away under guard.' Going at once to Jesus, Judas said, 'Rabbi!' and kissed him. The men seized Jesus and arrested him. Then one of those standing near drew his sword and struck the servant of the high priest, cutting off his ear.
>
> 'Am I leading a rebellion,' said Jesus, 'that you have come out with swords and clubs to capture me? Every day I was with you, teaching in the temple courts, and you did not arrest me. But the Scriptures must be fulfilled.' Then everyone deserted him and fled. (Mark 14: 43-50.)

Christ's death fulfilled all that the true and living God had promised in the Law and Prophets: He was mocked and ridiculed; physically assaulted; deserted by His disciples; rejected by the crowds; then condemned to die a horrendous death. The religious and political authorities – the whole world – conspired against Him:

---

38   Psalm 41: 9 cf John 13: 18

The whole assembly rose and led him off to Pilate. And they began to accuse him, saying, 'We have found this man subverting our nation. He opposes payment of taxes to Caesar and claims to be Messiah, a king.'

When [Pilate] learned that Jesus was under Herod's jurisdiction, he sent him to Herod, who was also in Jerusalem at that time. When Herod saw Jesus, he was greatly pleased, because for a long time he had been wanting to see him. From what he had heard about him, he hoped to see him perform a sign of some sort. He plied him with many questions, but Jesus gave him no answer. The chief priests and the teachers of the law were standing there, vehemently accusing him. Then Herod and his soldiers ridiculed and mocked him. Dressing him in an elegant robe, they sent him back to Pilate. That day Herod and Pilate became friends – before this they had been enemies. (Luke 23: 1-2, 7-12)

Herod and Pilate 'had been enemies' but they united in friendship to destroy the Son of God. Everyone wanted to rid the world of the LORD Jesus. Yet in doing so they only served to fulfil the plans of the true and living God. He was sovereign over their wickedness:

The God of Abraham, Isaac and Jacob, the God of our fathers, has glorified his servant Jesus. You handed him over to be killed, and you disowned him before Pilate, though he had decided to let him go. You disowned the Holy and Righteous One and asked that a murderer be released to you. You killed the author of life, but God raised him from the dead. We are witnesses of this. By faith in the name of Jesus, this man whom you see and know was made strong. It is Jesus' name and the faith that comes through him that has completely healed him, as you can all see. 'Now, fellow Israelites, I know that you acted in ignorance, as did your leaders. But this is how God fulfilled what he had foretold through all the prophets, saying that his Messiah would suffer. (Acts 3: 13-18)

Christ was nailed to the cross and killed by wicked men but He was handed over to them 'by God's deliberate plan and foreknowledge'.[39] Right to the end Christ trusted in His Father and submitted to His plan of salvation out of love for humanity. He did not abuse His persecutors; rather He asked His Father to forgive them.[40]

Yet however strong His faith in His Father, Christ still had to endure the pain and isolation of death: the awful moment when, out of the Triune God's love for humanity, the eternal loving relationship between the Father and Son in the Spirit was broken:

From noon until three in the afternoon darkness came over all the land. About three in the afternoon Jesus cried out in a loud voice, 'Eli, Eli, lema sabachthani?' (which means 'My God, my God, why have you forsaken me?'). [Psalm 22:1][41]

When some of those standing there heard this, they said, 'He's calling Elijah.' Immediately one of them ran and got a sponge. He filled it with wine vinegar, put it on a staff, and offered it to Jesus to drink. The rest said, 'Now leave him alone. Let's see if Elijah comes to save him.'

And when Jesus had cried out again in a loud voice, he gave up his spirit.

---

39 Acts 2: 22-24

40 Luke 23: 24.

41 Psalm 22: 1 to Psalm 31: 5 give us insight into Christ's thoughts whilst He hung on the cross.

> At that moment the curtain of the temple was torn in two from top to bottom. The earth shook, the rocks split and the tombs broke open. (Matthew 27: 45-52)

Even as Christ felt the weight of His alienation from His Father, He still trusted in Him. 'For as the curtain of the temple was torn in two, He called out with a loud voice, "Father, into your hands I commit my spirit". [Psalm 31:5] When He had said this, He breathed his last.' (Luke 23: 46)

Suffering brings Glory

Satan's mission seemed to be complete. The Son of God – the Seed of the Woman – was dead. Yet it was that death that defeated Satan's power and the power of all worldly authorities[42]. The Seed's heel had been struck, Satan had been crushed[43].

Having taken upon Himself the sin of humanity, Christ rose from the dead – His work on the cross was vindicated. He demonstrated in His risen body that He had conquered sin and death through His death. Through the resurrection, He was restored to relationship with His Father, fulfilling the great promise of the ancient Scriptures: 'You are my Son; today I have become your Father' (Psalm 2: 7)[44].

The risen Christ led the praise of His Father among the Church in celebration of His salvation from death.[45] Christ's suffering had turned to glory. It was exactly as had been prophesied, as He reminded His disciples after His resurrection:

---

42   Colossians 2: 15

43   Genesis 3: 15

44   See Acts 13: 33

45   Psalm 22: 22-24

Did not the Messiah have to suffer these things and then enter his glory?' And beginning with Moses and all the Prophets, [Jesus] explained to them what was said in all the Scriptures concerning himself.

...He said to them, 'This is what I told you while I was still with you: everything must be fulfilled that is written about me in the Law of Moses, the Prophets and the Psalms.' Then he opened their minds so they could understand the Scriptures. He told them, 'This is what is written: the Messiah will suffer and rise from the dead on the third day, and repentance for the forgiveness of sins will be preached in his name to all nations, beginning at Jerusalem. You are witnesses of these things. I am going to send you what my Father has promised; but stay in the city until you have been clothed with power from on high.' (Luke 24:26-27, 44-49))[46]

A little later, Christ ascended to heaven to sit at the right hand of His Father, reuniting God and man, and with authority over His enemies.

When this priest had offered for all time one sacrifice for sins, he sat down at the right hand of God, and since that time he waits for his enemies to be made his footstool. For by one sacrifice he has made perfect for ever those who are being made holy. (Hebrews 10: 12-14)[47]

[God the Father] raised Christ from the dead and seated him at his right hand in the heavenly realms, far above all rule and authority, power and dominion, and every name that is invoked, not only in the present age but also in the one to come. And God placed all things under his

---

46   See 1 Peter 1: 11

47   See Psalm 110: 1 and Psalm 8:4-6.

feet and appointed him to be head over everything for the church, which is his body, the fullness of him who fills everything in every way. (Ephesians 1: 20-23)

As the Scriptures had foretold, the Father lifted Christ up from His suffering to a position of authority and splendour:

And being found in appearance as a man, [Christ] humbled himself by becoming obedient to death – even death on a cross! God exalted him to the highest place and gave him the name that is above every name, that at the name of Jesus every knee should bow, in heaven and on earth and under the earth, and every tongue acknowledge that Jesus Christ is Lord, to the glory of God the Father. (Philippians 2:8-11)

Following His incarnation, Christ suffered the most terrible persecution; yet after His death, He rose again and ascended into heaven where He reigns in glory. Hallelujah!

CONCLUSION

'A TIME, TIMES AND HALF A TIME'

The Church's global mission

The LORD Jesus Christ has fulfilled what the Law and Prophets foretold about His suffering and glory. Sin and death have been defeated. The risen, ascended Christ sits at the right hand of the Father with everything under His feet[1], waiting for the Day when He will return to earth to eradicate all sin and death and make all things new. The Church also waits for that Day, longing for Her Bridegroom to appear.

As Christ waits, He works to bring more people into His Church – people from all over the world. The Prophets had looked forward to this time after Christ's ascension when the Church would have an *international* mission. The promise made to Abraham was that the gospel of Christ was for 'all nations'.[2] The Prophets testified that the Church would no longer reside in Israel as a witness to the surrounding nations; it was to spread out across the earth, dwelling in every country, witnessing to every people:

> Praise the Lord, all you nations; extol him, all you peoples. (Psalm 117:1).[3]

---

1   Psalm 8: 5-6, 1 Corinthians 15: 20-28

2   Genesis 12: 1-3, Galatians 3: 7-9.

3   See also 2 Samuel 22: 50, Psalm 18: 49, Deuteronomy 32: 43, Isaiah 11: 10, 52: 15, Amos 9: 11-12.

Before Christ had ascended to heaven, He had confirmed the truth of these ancient prophecies, calling His disciples to be His 'witnesses in Jerusalem, and in all Judea and Samaria, and to the ends of the earth' (Acts 1: 8)[4]. At Pentecost, the Church was equipped by the Holy Spirit for this global task of evangelism. Its task was – and remains – to proclaim Christ's name across the world, forming local congregations of believers in every nation. The return of the LORD is delayed so that, through His Church, He can bring more and more people to salvation:

> The LORD is not slow in keeping his promise [about the Second Coming], as some understand slowness. He is patient with you, not wanting anyone to perish, but everyone to come to repentance... But in keeping with his promise we are looking forward to a new heaven and a new earth, where righteousness dwells. So then, dear friends, since you are looking forward to this, make every effort to be found spotless, blameless and at peace with him. Bear in mind that our LORD's patience means salvation. (2 Peter 3: 9. 13-15)[5]

On-Going Persecution

As Christ began His work – through the Church – of proclaiming the gospel across the globe[6], His disciples were subject to great persecution[7]. Although defeated on the cross, the devil and the worldly powers have not given up their attacks on the LORD and His people. Christ has

---

4   See also Matthew 28: 16-20

5   See also Matthew 24: 14 and James 5: 7-8

6   The book of Acts makes clear that it records all that Christ *continued* to do after His ascension (Acts 1: 1-2)

7   Acts 4: 1-22, 5: 17-42 6: 8-15, 7: 54-60, 8:1, 11: 19, 13: 50 etc

won the war over Satan but until the devil's power has been completely eliminated from the world, casualties must continue to be expected.

Christ had made clear when He prepared His disciples for their global mission that they must expect persecution. It was inevitable that the world would treat them in the same way it treated Him: Christ and His body were inseparable:

> Whoever listens to you listens to me; whoever rejects you rejects me (Luke 10: 16)[1]

> If the world hates you, keep in mind that it hated me first. If you belonged to the world, it would love you as its own. As it is, you do not belong to the world, but I have chosen you out of the world. That is why the world hates you. Remember what I told you: "A servant is not greater than his master." [John 13:16] If they persecuted me, they will persecute you also. If they obeyed my teaching, they will obey yours also. They will treat you this way because of my name, for they do not know the one who sent me. If I had not come and spoken to them, they would not be guilty of sin; but now they have no excuse for their sin. Whoever hates me hates my Father as well. If I had not done among them the works no one else did, they would not be guilty of sin. As it is, they have seen, and yet they have hated both me and my Father. But this is to fulfil what is written in their Law: "They hated me without reason." [Psalms 35:19; 69: 4] (John 15: 18-25)[2]

In the parable of the sower and the soil, Christ made clear that persecution tests whether someone really is one of His followers:

---

1   cf Acts 9:4

2   See also Matthew 24: 3-9

Then Jesus said to [the crowd], 'Don't you understand this parable? How then will you understand any parable? The farmer sows the word. Some people are like seed along the path, where the word is sown. As soon as they hear it, Satan comes and takes away the word that was sown in them. Others, like seed sown on rocky places, hear the word and at once receive it with joy. But since they have no root, they last only a short time. **When trouble or persecution comes because of the word, they quickly fall away.** Still others, like seed sown among thorns, hear the word; but the worries of this life, the deceitfulness of wealth and the desires for other things come in and choke the word, making it unfruitful. Others, like seed sown on good soil, hear the word, accept it, and produce a crop – some thirty, some sixty, some a hundred times what was sown.' (Mark 4: 13-20).[3]

When persecution came – as it inevitably would – Christ's disciples must stand firm. The Triune God would look after His people when they faced persecution. The LORD Jesus prayed that the Father would protect His disciples from the evil one as He sent them out into the world with His Word – and Christ continues to pray for them in their time of need[4]. They will not be left alone:

On my account you will be brought before governors and kings as witnesses to them and to the Gentiles. But when they arrest you, do not worry about what to say or how to say it. At that time you will be given what to say, for it will not be you speaking, but the Spirit of your

---

3   See also Mark 8: 34-37. The apostle Paul echoed his Master's words, saying, 'Everyone who wants to live a godly life in Christ Jesus will be persecuted'. (2 Timothy 3: 12)

4   John 17: 13-19. Hebrews 4: 14-16.

> Father speaking through you. Brother will betray brother to death, and a father his child; children will rebel against their parents and have them put to death. You will be hated by everyone because of me, but the one who stands firm to the end will be saved. (Matthew 10: 18-22)

Those who have taken up their cross for Christ will earn a great reward:

> Jesus said to [His disciples], 'Truly I tell you, at the renewal of all things, when the Son of Man sits on his glorious throne, you who have followed me will also sit on twelve thrones, judging the twelve tribes of Israel. And everyone who has left houses or brothers or sisters or father or mother or wife or children or fields for my sake will receive a hundred times as much and will inherit eternal life. But many who are first will be last, and many who are last will be first. (Matthew 19: 28-30)[5]

Suffering and Glory

The Church suffered terribly in the days after Christ ascended to His Father; yet it was also very fruitful and multiplied greatly.[6] The Triune God used the persecution of the Church to promote its growth by scattering the followers of Christ across the world, taking the gospel beyond

5 The apostle Paul again echoes his LORD's words when saying, 'If we are children, then we are heirs – heirs of God and co-heirs with Christ, if indeed we share in his sufferings in order that we may also share in his glory. I consider that our present sufferings are not worth comparing with the glory that will be revealed in us.' (Romans 8: 17-18). Peter has a similar message: 'Dear friends, do not be surprised at the fiery ordeal that has come on you to test you, as though something strange were happening to you. But rejoice inasmuch as you participate in the sufferings of Christ, so that you may be overjoyed when his glory is revealed. If you are insulted because of the name of Christ, you are blessed, for the Spirit of glory and of God rests on you.' (1 Peter 4: 12-14)

6 Acts 2: 24, 47, 4: 4, 16: 5, 19: 20

Jerusalem into other lands.[7] One of the people who led the persecution of the Church (Saul) was converted (becoming Paul) and then became the key player in taking the gospel to the Gentiles, facing tremendous persecution himself.[8]

The Church continues to multiply today, and it continues to be persecuted. As the Church proclaims Christ as LORD it will inevitably face attack from those believing in other lords. The Church's testimony that Jesus is LORD is good news to many – yet a stumbling block to those who trust in other lords. And they take out their hatred of Christ on His ambassadors.

As you read this, many people are coming to know Jesus as their LORD and Saviour; and many Christians are being persecuted – by political authorities; economic powers; religious authorities[9]; and their own families.

The Triune God has entrusted the task of protecting the local congregations of believers to the governments of the world, so that His disciples may be free to undertake their gospel work.[10] Yet these rulers are powerless to stop all the persecution that takes place. Political authorities cannot prevent sin; moreover, they are infected by it themselves. It is often governments which are the ones persecuting the Church, neglecting their task of protecting it.

Christians have been persecuted since the time of Abel

---

7   Acts 8: 1-4, 11: 19.

8   The Lord says of Saul/Paul after his conversion: 'This man is my chosen instrument to proclaim my name to the Gentiles and their kings and to the people of Israel. I will show him how much he must suffer for my name' (Acts 9: 15-16).

9   In John 16: 1-3, the LORD warned His disciples about those who will try to kill them in the belief that 'they are offering a service to God', even though they do not know God at all – the Father revealed by the Son through the Spirit.

10   1 Timothy 2: 1-4

but this suffering will not last forever. The prophet Daniel foretold that the people of God must endure suffering for 'a time, times and half a time' and then the power of the world's kingdoms will be overcome by the Messiah and His kingdom will be established forever[11]. The suffering will continue for 'a time' but a glorious end is in sight when Christ comes to institute the new creation: 'The name of the LORD will be declared in Zion and his praise in Jerusalem when the peoples and the kingdoms assemble to worship the LORD' (Psalm 102: 21-22) and 'the sound of weeping and of crying will be heard in it no more' (Isaiah 65: 19)[12].

In the time in which we wait for that Day, Christians will suffer at the hands of those who hate the LORD Jesus. But the Triune God does not leave us to suffer alone. He responds to our prayers and speaks to us through the Scriptures to help us cope with our persecution: warning us, comforting us, and giving us hope, encouragement and strength by fixing our eyes on Christ. In particular, He has given us the Law and the Prophets which testify to Christ, and on which He and His apostles grounded their sermons and writings.[13]

As this book has shown, the Old Testament prophets have much to teach us about enduring persecution. In summary:

1. The gospel of Christ is the gospel of suffering. Since Adam, the world has forsaken the true and living God.

---

11 Daniel chapters 7 and 12. See also Revelation 11: 1-14 and 12: 1-17.

12 cf Revelation 21:1-4

13 See Acts 4: 23-31; Romans 8: 31-39, 12: 14-21. The apostle Paul testified, when subject to arrest by a king, that 'I am saying nothing beyond what the prophets and Moses said would happen – that the Messiah would suffer and, as the first to rise from the dead, would bring the message of light to his own people and to the Gentiles.' (Acts 26: 22-23).

Yet Christ took that God-forsakenness upon Himself through His suffering on the cross, enabling humanity to have eternal life with the true and living God. Anyone can relate to the holy God Most High because of the death, resurrection and ascension of Christ.

2. Those who follow the LORD Jesus Christ and proclaim Him to be the One Way to God must also expect to suffer.

3. The LORD suffers when His people suffer. When His Body hurts, He hurts. He empathises with their suffering because of His suffering.

4. When Christians are persecuted, they can pray to God Most High through the LORD Jesus Christ about their suffering. He wants them to tell Him about their pain and fears.

5. The governments of the world are instituted by God the Father, Son and Spirit to protect His Church, although rulers often collude with or actively promote its persecution.

6. The Triune God will protect His people when they are being persecuted – either by intervening to stop their suffering or by seeing them through death. Those who follow Christ have no fear of death – which robs their persecutors of their power.

7. He will judge those who persecute His people. The empires of the world may look powerful, but their reign is temporary.

8. Knowing that the Triune God will deal justly with their enemies, His people are to repay evil not with evil but with good.

9. Whatever the suffering of Christians now, they can look forward to a glorious future in the new creation with God the Father, Son and Holy Spirit. In their future home, there will be no sin or death or suffering.

May we follow the example of the Old Testament prophets; may we rejoice in the light of our sufferings, and be patient and stand firm until the glorious coming of the LORD Jesus. For the glory of God the Father, Son and Holy Spirit.